W9-BNS-946

Learning Language Arts through Literature

THE PURPLE BOOK

By

Debbie Strayer and Susan Simpson

Common Sense Press
™

The *Learning Language Arts through Literature* Series:

The Blue Book - 1st Grade Skills
The Red Book - 2nd Grade Skills
The Yellow Book - 3rd Grade Skills
The Orange Book - 4th Grade Skills
The Purple Book - 5th Grade Skills
The Tan Book - 6th Grade Skills
The Green Book - 7th-8th Grade Skills
The Gray Book - 8th-9th Grade Skills
The Gold Book - High School Skills

Copyright ©1994 by:

Common Sense Press
8786 Highway 21
P.O. Box 1365
Melrose, FL 32666
(904) 475-5757

All rights reserved. No part of this book may be reproduced in any form without written permission from Common Sense Press.

Printed in the United States of America.

ISBN 1-880892-36-7

Introduction

As parents we watched and marveled at the way our little ones learned to talk. By listening and responding to English spoken well, they were able to communicate quite clearly. The process was so gradual that they were not even aware it was taking place.

It is the belief of those associated with the *Learning Language Arts through Literature* series that written language can best be learned in the same manner. By reading fine literature and working with good models of writing, children will receive a quality education in language arts. If you desire to teach using this integrated approach to language, this curriculum is for you.

In her books, Dr. Ruth Beechick has confirmed that this method of teaching is an appropriate and successful way to introduce our students to the joys of reading, writing and thinking. Our own experiences using these lessons with children have encouraged us to share them with you. Their enjoyment and enthusiasm for reading and writing is an unmatched recommendation for this method of teaching.

How To Use This Book

This book provides materials, activities and suggestions that will encourage and benefit you as you create a learning environment for your family. Since all families vary, we suggest that you try our ideas and then freely experiment until you find patterns that work for your family.

Let us first introduce *Learning Language Arts through Literature*. After this introduction you will find the following:

Lessons: The lessons contain passages of literature, as well as several full length selections to be read by you and your student. Learning activities are contained in each lesson. These activities are designed to help your students learn language skills in their context while developing writing, thinking and speaking skills. An emphasis is placed on learning and applying writing skills appropriate for the upper elementary grades. In each lesson the student will either copy the passage of literature or take it from dictation.

When copying the passage, we suggest allowing your student to use the Student Editing Model. Copying material is a very powerful learning activity. It trains a student to look for details, strive for accuracy, and learn the process of writing. After he has made his first copy, ask him to check it with the model and make any needed corrections.

When dictation is used in the lesson, you will need to clearly read the passage sentence by sentence using your voice and pauses to indicate punctuation marks needed. An optional dictation tape is available for your convenience.

Since this method may be new for you, here are a few suggestions:

1. Before dictation or copying, read the entire passage to your student while he listens only.
2. Begin the dictation by reading one sentence at a time. If necessary repeat the sentence, reading it one phrase at a time.
3. Instruct your student to leave a blank line between each written line so that corrections can be made more easily.
4. After dictation or copying, allow your student to use the Student Model to edit his own work. At first have him check his work one line or phrase at a time. After each line or phrase has been corrected, move to the next one until all the work is correct. Asking him to correct all work at once may prove to be frustrating for him.

An audio tape has been made available containing the majority of the dictation passages.

This tape can be used to help your student develop auditory perceptual skills, as well as to become familiar with the process of writing from dictation.

The units are written in numbered lessons for easy reference. A lesson can take one to two weeks to complete, depending on you and your student. The units may be completed as listed in this manual, or changed to meet your schooling needs.

Teacher Helps at the end of each lesson give answers to questions in that lesson.

Student Editing Models: Following the lessons, is a section entitled **Student Editing Models**. So your children may easily correct their own writing, we have included each literature passage, labeled by lesson number, and typed in large print. These models may also be used when your child is copying or editing a passage.

Appendix: The next section, the **Appendix**, contains longer literature selections, illustrations, maps, etc. to be used in the lessons.

Language Arts Skills Index: The **Language Arts Skills Index** follows next in this manual. To ensure that skills commonly held to be appropriate for fifth grade instruction were adequately covered, much research was involved in the writing of this book. This information was primarily gleaned from these sources: *You CAN Teach Your Child Successfully* by Ruth Beechick and *Teaching Children: A Curriculum Guide to What Children Need to Know at Each Level Through Sixth Grade* by Diane Lopez.

If your child has a particularly strong or weak area, you can easily locate lessons that will address specific skills using the Skills Index. If your child receives standardized testing, skills listed on the test may be found in the Skills Index.

Bibliography: Next you will find the **Bibliography**. This will give you all the information you need to locate the books quoted in the lessons. The selection includes wonderful books that we hope your family will read and enjoy.

An Integrated Language Approach

Grammar, vocabulary, writing mechanics, reading, spelling, penmanship and thinking, listening and speaking skills are all taught using these lessons. This section contains many suggestions for making these subjects beneficial to your student and providing a successful experience for him in language arts. We suggest you reread the following sections periodically throughout your school year.

This integrated language arts program offers the benefits of a holistic approach, plus the advantages of the basal methods as well. By working with whole pieces of literature and focusing on the skills, your student has the best possible advantage for learning skills in an effective and lasting manner.

GRAMMAR

We believe that grammar should be taught in the midst of writing, not as an isolated subject. You may find it helpful to have a grammar textbook for reference. We suggest *Learning Grammar Through Writing*. This inexpensive paperback is simple to use with clearly presented rules and examples, each one numbered for each reference. The grammar sections in the lessons are correlated with *Learning Grammar Through Writing*. Numbered rules and examples for this book are referenced in the Teacher Helps.

As your student works on his lessons you will evaluate his progress by his success in the activities. If you believe he needs more time on specific activities for that week we suggest you locate your own passage of literature and use the same learning activities. If one concept seems to present difficulty you may add that to each lesson for several weeks. For example: if recognizing nouns is a problem, your student may circle the nouns in red each week.

During the writing activities in this program, we suggest you focus on the grammatical concepts that are difficult for your student. Remember that the purpose of grammar study is to help the student become a better writer. So good writing equals a good grammar study.

VOCABULARY

Your student's vocabulary will be enhanced by reading good literature, as well as by discussion. Reading the classics aloud together is an excellent vocabulary building activity. When a new word is found, be sure to wait until the end of that passage to discuss the new word. Use the opportunity of a new word to help your student decipher the word using the context. As your student works with good literature on a regular basis, he will develop a larger vocabulary and an ear for proper word and sentence usage.

In this manual new words are introduced and the student is asked to write a definition from a dictionary. The purpose of this is to encourage the student to recognize that words are tools available for his use. As he encounters a word, sees its proper usage, defines it and uses it in the activities, he has acquired that word as a tool. Enabling the student to see the "tools" in his toolbox will build his confidence and ability to use our language effectively. In writing definitions, we are not suggesting that the student copy verbatim, but rather that he read the definition, discuss it with the teacher and write a definition that is accurate and meaningful to the student.

PENMANSHIP

We recommend the section entitled "Penmanship", pages 124-132, in Ruth Beechick's book *You CAN Teach Your Child Successfully* as a basis for your instruction. Since skill in handwriting is influenced by maturity in fine motor ability, improvement from what-ever point the student begins is the goal. If it is necessary for you to assign grades from handwriting, we suggest you compare the student's present handwriting with his initial handwriting. Comparing his handwriting to an artificial standard can be discouraging for all concerned. Concentrating on many skills at once (writing, reading directions and grammar) can be a frustrating experience, so we suggest evaluation of handwriting be done only on final copies of written activities. Correction of handwriting errors should be done by focusing on one or two errors at a time. Correcting all formation errors at one time is overwhelming and ineffective. Cursive handwriting instruction is also suc-cessful to varying degrees based on perceptual motor maturity. Follow your student's pace in introducing cursive and in requiring cursive usage. If cursive is difficult for your student, it is best to require his best handwriting only in short assignments, or by taking several days to complete a long written assignment.

When your student is working on a creative writing activity, it is important to let him write rough drafts and brainstorming ideas with no concern for neatness, other than his ability to read what he has written. Many fifth graders will want to compose orally, and will need the teacher's assistance writing rough drafts and note-taking. It is always beneficial to discuss the student's thoughts as he is formulating them, and through this process you will enable him to put his thoughts in order for writing.

READING

We realize that each child will function at a different reading level. For the child who is a reluctant reader, we recommend several steps in strengthening his reading ability:

1. Read the passages to your child. Use the Student Editing Models for this purpose.
2. Ask your child to read the passage silently, pointing out unknown words. After this reading, ask him to read it to you.
3. Spend time reviewing any difficult words, phonics concepts that need review and sight words or "exceptions" that are difficult for your student.
4. During the course of the lesson, you may want to repeat this process. Your student can listen as you read, or listen to the taped passage. He may want to read the passage on tape and then listen to himself read. This may be very helpful in building reading confidence.

These steps may be used in one day or in one week. The most important aspect in the reading of the passages for your child is to be successful. PLEASE do not pressure your child to get every word right, as though it was a test he was taking for you. Instead use mistakes or problems in the reading process as an opportunity to teach a skill or to provide the encouragement needed for success.

Getting sufficient reading practice seems to be a concern to some. If your student is reading frequently in other content areas as well as reading for pleasure, additional reading practice is not necessarily needed. However, if you feel additional practice is required, choose material 1or your student that is interesting, and on a level that allows for comprehension. Decoding many words detracts from understanding and enjoyment. We recommend the *Reading Skills Discovery Series*. Study guides have been developed for the books *Caddie Woodlawn, Sarah, Plain and Tall, Wheel on the School* and *Wilbur and Orville Wright*. We also recommend the *Bookshelf Collection* Series, which provides book report alternatives for several quality children's books. These provide discussion activities and additional reading and comprehension practice in an appropriate, effective and enjoyable manner. This practice would eliminate the need for any additional workbook-type activities.

SPELLING

In her book *You CAN Teach Your Child Successfully*, Ruth Beechick describes three approaches to teaching spelling. She describes the common word approach, which textbooks use to make lists of most commonly used words. The second approach to spelling is the phonics approach, where lists are based on phonetic patterns and spelling rules. The third approach consists of spelling lists made up of words your student misspells in his writing.

Based on the above information, we recommend several methods for teaching spelling.

1. Observe your student during the reading and writing of the activities to identify five or six words that are difficult for him. As you work with the activities you can highlight these words. Identify vowel sounds, silent letters, base words, prefixes and suffixes, or any other distinctive aspect of the words as you work with them.
2. After the final dictation or test taken at the end of all activities on a passage or topic, any misspelled words (up to six) may be added to the teacher's master list of spelling words for the student. These words can be used as a spelling list for the following week. Using this method, the date of mastery is written on the master list by the teacher. Again, evaluation of the mastery may be determined by observation, a spelling test or use of the word in dictation or writing. It may take several weeks for a word to be mastered by your student. The master list may be reviewed periodically.

Be sure to incorporate all four modalities in spelling learning: reading the word, writing the word, spelling the word orally and listening to the word being read and spelled. If your child seems proficient at spelling, enrichment or challenge words should be drawn (no more than 5 a week) from other content areas (particularly science or history) or Dr. Beechick's word lists.

If you feel you need further guidelines for spelling, we recommend Ruth Beechick's book.

THINKING SKILLS

Thinking skills are developed throughout the activities in this manual. Anytime a student is asked to respond to the literature with discussion, writing, drawing or completing an activity, your student is developing his thinking skills. This is particularly evident when writing is involved. Writing sentences describing how he would solve a problem will be a challenge to your student. It is very important for you to discuss your student's thoughts with him, providing the help and structure he needs to be successful in his task. As he becomes comfortable with the demands of creative thinking/writing, encourage him to work on a rough draft, editing and rewriting as he thinks and talks with you about the assignment. All writers must go through this process of ordering and recording their thoughts, so be encouraging and patient as your student learns to think and write well. Verbal skills as well as listening skills are also a very important part of your student's abilities, and are also developed through the activities described in the lessons.

MATERIALS TO USE

To use the manual you will need pencils, paper, colored pencils, drawing paper, a notebook, file folders and construction paper. Frequently in the lessons, the student must find a book he is familiar with, so children's books (either your own books or library books) are needed from time to time.

Previous lessons are often used again, so keep all the student's work until the entire unit is completed.

Reference books, such as a dictionary or thesaurus will be used as well as encyclopedias. Availability of these materials in either the home or library is adequate.

Additional Resources Mentioned

Learning Grammar Through Writing, by Sandra M. Bell and James I. Wheeler, ©1984. Published by Educators Publishing Service, Inc., 75 Moulton Street, Cambridge, MA 02138. (Cost is approximately $11.00, available from many curriculum suppliers.)

LESSONS

LESSON 1

America
by Samuel Francis Smith (1808-1895)

My country, 'tis of thee.
Sweet land of liberty,
Of thee I sing;
Land where my fathers died,
Land of the Pilgrims' pride,
From every mountain side
Let Freedom ring.

DAY 1

A. Listen as your teacher reads this poem to you. After your teacher reads it aloud a second time, look over the poem and point out any words that are unfamiliar to you. After making sure you know all the words, read this poem aloud to your teacher.

B. This poem describes America in three ways. The descriptions are easy to find because they each include the word "land." Find these three descriptions and read them to your teacher.

All of these descriptions talk about our heritage, or history. Talk with your teacher about the answer to these three questions regarding our history.

1. From what do you think our country provided liberty?
2. Who do you think the poem means by "my fathers"?
3. According to the poem what was the Pilgrims' attitude toward America?

C. Talk with your teacher about the ways Americans remember the events and people of our history. Talking with your teacher, come up with a list of ways we remember our beginnings as a nation, and the people who have worked to help establish our country. Here are some ideas to get started: holidays, songs, names of cities, etc.

DAY 2

A. Words can be broken down into syllables. A syllable consists of one of the following:

a vowel sound

      example: "a" in about = a/bout

a vowel sound with consonant sounds before it

      example: "fa" in fathers = fa/thers

a vowel sound with consonant sounds after it

      example: "er" in liberty = lib/er/ty

a vowel sound with consonant sounds surrounding it

      example: "dom" in Freedom = Free/dom

The key to finding syllables is to look for vowel sounds and determine what, if any, consonant sounds go with them.

Accented syllables are spoken more loudly than unaccented syllables. The word "chicken," for example, has two separate vowel sounds, so there are two syllables. The consonants that go with the vowel sounds make the syllables chick/en. When we say "chicken," the syllable chick is loud and sharp, but the "en" is soft. Therefore, the accent is on "chick" and "en" is unaccented. To show this, we use marks over the syllables that look like this: "chick′ ĕn."

B. Look at each line of the first verse of *America,* by Samuel Francis Smith. These lines can be divided into syllables, and the syllables can be marked accented or unaccented. First, count the number of syllables in each line. Next, mark the syllables accented or unaccented. Do you see a pattern? This pattern, in poetry, is called "meter."

C. Read the verse again, using the marks as your pronunciation guide. Read the accented syllables with greater emphasis than the unaccented syllables. It may sound very awkward at first, so practice reading several times.

DAY 3

A. A possessive noun shows that something belongs to someone. Here is an example:

This is Bob's book.

("Bob's" is the possessive noun. The book belongs to Bob.)

Read each of these sentences and tell your teacher what belongs to whom.

1. Where are Dad's car keys?
2. Give me the dog's dish.
3. Look at the bird's nest.

Each one of these sentences tells us about a noun, or a naming word, that belongs to someone or something. There is only one owner, so we call these singular possessive nouns. Using your name, write three sentences that tell about things that belong to you. Use an 's to show that the things belong to you. For example:

Mrs. Strayer's hair is brown.

B. When there is more than one owner of something, we call it a plural possessive noun. Here are some examples:

1. Here comes the boys' dog.
2. Where is the Smiths' house?
3. Did you like the trees' color?

Look at the possessive noun that has the apostrophe (') added to it in the first sentence. What do you notice about the apostrophe when the noun is plural and ends with an s? Can you make up a rule that tells how to make plural nouns possessive or the owners of something?

C. In our passage there is a phrase that tells us about something belonging to the Pilgrims. Find it and show it to your teacher.

Write three sentences that tell about things that belong to everyone in your family. Remember, when there is more than one owner of something, we usually put an apostrophe after the s to make the word a plural possessive noun. For example:

The Strayers' car is tan.

DAY 4

Listen as your teacher reads the excerpt from the book *Patriotic Songs* (found in the Appendix), part of the *Color the Classics* series. This excerpt tells about the song *America* and its author, Samuel Francis Smith. After listening to your teacher read, answer the following questions orally.

1. Why do you think Samuel Francis Smith was interested in the ride of Paul Revere? What did he find out about it?
2. Where did Samuel go to college? What did he decide to do after college?
3. When did Samuel write *America?* When was it first performed?

A. It is wonderful to memorize poetry. There are other things that are good to memorize as well, such as Scriptures. Memorizing something is not that hard, it just takes practice.

Read your poem silently. Reread the first three lines, either silently or out loud. Read the first three lines again out loud. Now look away, or close your eyes, and repeat the first three lines. If you get stuck, open your eyes, find the word you need and then go on to the end of those three lines. Keep doing this until you feel sure you know them.

B. Now add the next two lines and repeat the process we described in Part A of this lesson. Continue until you are finished, then repeat the two parts together. Finally add the last two lines using the same process. You will need to practice more than one time to really be able to remember it. The best way to remember it is to practice for a few minutes a couple of times a day.

C. When you have the poem memorized, say it for your family. By now you may know that this is also a song, so you may want to sing it for your family instead. Once you have presented it on your own (either by speaking or singing) ask your family to join in and do it with you the second time.

Teacher Helps:

Day 1 B.   Sweet land...
        Land where...
        Land of...

        3. The pilgrims felt pride toward America.

Day 2 B.

My coun try 'tis of thee,   6

Sweet land of lib er ty,   6

Of thee I sing;   4

Land where my fa thers died,   6

Land of the Pil grims pride,   6

From eve ry moun tain side   6

Let Free dom ring.   4

Day 3 A.   The car keys that belong to dad.
The dish that belongs to the dog.
The nest that belongs to the bird.

For further explanation of possessive nouns, see *Learning Grammar Through Writing,* 1h.

B.   The dog that belongs to the boys.
The house that belongs to the Smiths.
The color belonging to the trees.

The apostrophe follows the s.
When a plural noun ends in an s, we make it possessive by putting the apostrophe after the s.

C.   Land of the Pilgrims' pride.

Day 4   1. Answers will vary.
2. Samuel went to Harvard. He then decided to become a pastor.
3. Samuel wrote *America* while translating music books from German to English for Lowell Mason. It was first performed on July 4, 1831.

LESSON 2

(verse 4)

Our fathers' God, to Thee,
Author of liberty,
To Thee we sing;
Long may our land be bright
With Freedom's holy light;
Protect us by Thy might,
Great God, our King.

DAY 1

A. In this verse of *America* there are many important words that describe what Americans believe. Two of these words are "liberty" and "freedom." Look these words up in the dictionary. Read the definitions to your teacher. Talk with your teacher about what each word means, and then write a definition for each word that tells what you know about each word. Don't just copy what is in the dictionary; put the meaning in your own words. Now that you have written a definition for the words "freedom" and "liberty," use each of the words in a sentence orally.

B. Citizenship in America assures us of certain freedoms, like those described in the Bill of Rights. Look in an encyclopedia or in the Appendix to find the ten Amendments that make up the Bill of Rights. After reading them or listening as your teacher reads them*, make a list of some of the freedoms we have as Americans. The list does not need to consist of complete sentences, just descriptions.

C. Look over the list you made of the freedoms listed in the Bill of Rights. Choose one of the freedoms. Talk with your teacher about how you think your life would be different if that freedom were taken away. Write a two or three sentence description of how things would change. You may want to think about and talk about the effects of several different freedoms being lost. You are only required to write about one.

---

* This is on the optional Dictation Tape.

DAY 2

A. A rhyme consists of two words in which the end sounds of the words are alike. In poetry, two lines are said to rhyme if the words at the ends of the lines rhyme. Look at the first verse of *America*, by Samuel Francis Smith found in Lesson 1. Look at the end word of line one and mark it "a." Look for all the words that rhyme with "thee," and mark them with an "a." Look at the end word of line three and mark it "b." Find the words that rhyme with "sing" and mark them with a "b." Now, mark the end word of line four with a "c." Find the end words that rhyme with "died" and mark them with a "c." This is called the "rhyme scheme" of the poem. In this case, the rhyme scheme is - a a b c c c b.

B. Now use the same process to mark the lines in verse 4 of *America*, found in this lesson. What is the rhyme scheme of verse four?

C. Write a series of words with the same rhyme scheme as used in *America*.

   Example: best, rest, day, night, light, sight, play

DAY 3

A. It is important to understand who the speaker is in this poem, and to whom the speaker is talking. Let's start by deciding to whom we are speaking. Read over the poem, either orally or silently and tell your teacher who you think "Thee" is in verse 4. Who is the speaker in this poem?

B. Now that we know who is talking, and to whom you are talking, we can identify the pronouns that are being used. Pronouns are words that replace nouns. They are naming words. The pronoun in the first sentence of verse 4 of *America* is "our." It replaces the name of our ancestors and shows that something belongs to them. Find the other pronouns in the verse that describe the American people. Point them out to your teacher.

C. On Day 3 of Lesson 1, we learned about singular and plural possessive nouns. Reread that section of the lesson if you are unsure of what it said.

In this verse, there are two examples of possessive nouns. Find them and show them to your teacher. One of these examples is singular, and one is plural. Tell your teacher which is singular, and which is plural, and how you can tell the difference.

D. If you would like, try to write a poem with the same rhyme scheme and meter as used in *America*. You may use your rhyming words from Day 2.

Example:

My poodle is the best
at getting lots of rest.
He sleeps all day.
When I lie down at night
my dog turns on the light.
He keeps me in his sight.
He wants to play.

DAY 4

Reread the excerpt of the book *Patriotic Songs* regarding the song *America*, found in the Appendix. You may read the excerpt silently or out loud to your teacher.

This poem reflected Samuel's love of our patriotic history. As a young boy, he was very interested in the ride of Paul Revere. Read about Paul Revere in an encyclopedia or history book and tell your teacher why this ride was such an important part of our history. Why do you think Samuel thought it was so exciting?

You may also want to listen as your teacher reads* *Paul Revere's Ride,* (found in the Appendix) which is a poem by Henry Wadsworth Longfellow. You may also want to color the illustration of Samuel thinking about the ride of Paul Revere (found in the Appendix).

DAY 5

We have spent two weeks studying verses from Samuel Francis Smith's poem *America*. Using the procedure outlined on Day 5 of Lesson 1, memorize this last verse of the poem. When you have learned this verse, combine it with the verse you memorized last week, and present the poem (either by speaking or singing) to your family, or you may want to memorize the poem you wrote this week and present it to your family.

We often only learn one or two verses of a poem or song, missing the beautiful and meaningful language of the other verses. The entire song, *America,* can be found in the

* This is on the optional Dictation Tape.

Appendix. Listen as your teacher reads the entire song to you.* What meaning did the other verses add to your understanding of Smith's poem *America*? You may want to try to memorize and present all four verses of this poem to your family.

Teacher Helps:

Day 2 B.   a a b c c c b

Day 3 A.   God
The person reading the poem. In this case, it's *you*.

    B.   we, our, us, our
For further explanation of pronouns, see *Learning Grammar Through Writing,* 1m.

    C.   Our fathers' God, Freedom's holy light.

One has an apostrophe after the s, fathers' God, meaning that God belongs to more than one father. Freedom's holy light is singular because freedom, as an owner of holy light, is singular, and the apostrophe comes before the s.

Day 4   Paul Revere's ride was important because it warned the people of the English invasion.

LESSON 3

Mr. Popper's Penguins
by Richard & Florence Atwater

Next day the picture of Mr. Popper and Captain Cook appeared in the Stillwater *Morning Chronicle*, with a paragraph about the house painter who had received a penguin by air express from Admiral Drake in the faraway Antarctic. Then the Associated Press picked up the story, and a week later the photograph, in rotogravure, could be seen in the Sunday edition of the most important newspapers in all the large cities in the country.

Naturally, the Poppers all felt very proud and happy.

From *Mr. Popper's Penguins* by Richard and Florence Atwater. Copyright ©1938 by Florence Atwater and Richard Atwater; © renewed 1966 by Florence Atwater, Doris Atwater, and Carroll Atwater Bishop. By permission of Little, Brown and Company.

DAY 1

A. Read the passage silently. Ask your teacher to help you with difficult words. When you are ready, read the passage out loud to your teacher. In your own words, tell your teacher what is happening in this passage.

B. As your teacher reads the lines in bold print out loud,* write them down. Compare your copy to the passage on this page and make corrections.

NOTE TO THE TEACHER: Spelling lists will be made of unknown words, misspelled words from dictation, and any unknown words from the word study activities. Please do not make weekly lists of more than 5 words. Keep track of words you do not cover and add them to later lists. Keep a list of these words from week to week, noting when they are mastered. Sheets for this purpose are found in the Appendix of this book and in the Student Activity Book.

DAY 2

A. Read the second paragraph of the passage to your teacher. That is an example of a complete sentence. Look at that sentence and tell your teacher what you remember about sentences? What is the subject in this sentence? What is the predicate in this sentence?

*This is on the optional Dictation Tape.

10

B. Pretend an animal—any animal—is delivered to your house by mistake. The zoo keeper says he can't pick up the animal until tomorrow, so you have to care for it for one day. Luckily, the animal comes with a leash.

Discuss this situation with your teacher. You might wonder where you will keep the animal, or what to feed it. Will you be able to play with it? What if the neighbors see it?

After your discussion, write five or six sentences, or much more if you like, summarizing the story of the day a zoo animal was delivered to your house by mistake.

Draw a picture which best illustrates your story.

DAY 3

A. Look at the passage again. There are many words in the passage which start with a capital letter. Every time we see a capital letter, an imaginary bell should ring in our minds. That bell reminds us that we should think about why the word starts with a capital letter. The capital letter gives us information that will help us understand what we are reading. Using a colored pencil or a highlighter marker, underline or mark all the words on your copy of the passage that begin with a capital letter.

B. Each of the words is capitalized for a reason. Here are several reasons why words are capitalized.

NOTE TO THE TEACHER: Write the following reasons on index cards or cut them out of your Purple Student Activity Book.

1. Use a capital letter to begin a sentence.

2. Use a capital letter to begin the names of holidays, months and days.

3. Use a capital letter when writing the names of places, like streets, towns or countries.

4. Use a capital letter to begin the name of a business or organization.

5. Use a capital letter to begin a person's or pet's name. All of a person's names (first, middle, and last name) are capitalized.

6. Use a capital letter to begin the first word and each important word in the titles of books, newspapers, movies, works of art or other titles.

C. Match the capital words that are highlighted in the passage to the reasons they are capitalized. Write the words on the back of the correct cards. This gives you at least one example of each reason. Keep these cards. We will use them again later, and add a few more reasons to capitalize.

DAY 4

A. In the passage, there are two words that mean about the same thing. Find the word "photograph" in your passage and draw a circle around it. There is another word in our passage that has about the same meaning. Find it and circle it. Words that are close in meaning are called synonyms.

B. Pick three words from the passage and look them up in a thesaurus. Reading the synonyms for each word, choose the one that is closest in meaning to the word in the passage.

C. Read the sentences again, replacing the words with the synonyms you chose. How do the sentences sound to you now? Is the meaning the same? When you are having trouble thinking of the right word to use when you are writing, a thesaurus may be a big help.

DAY 5

A. Listen as your teacher reads the first sentence of the passage.* You will now write this passage from dictation. Do not write as it is read the first time. Just listen. Remember, writing from dictation is a skill you acquire with practice, like hitting a baseball. Your first attempts may not be too successful, but as you practice you will become better.

B. After you listen to the passage the second time, write what you have heard. When you have finished, compare your copy to the passage at the beginning of this lesson.

C. Listen as your teacher dictates the spelling words you have been learning this week. Write each word as your teacher reads it to you. After you write each word, use it in a sentence orally. When you are finished, compare your spellings to the correct spellings on your list, and make any needed corrections.

NOTE TO THE TEACHER: Be sure to add correctly spelled words to a master list that you keep for each student. Record the date the words are correctly spelled.

* This is on the optional Dictation Tape.

Teacher Helps:

Day 2 A.   begin with a capital letter
end with a punctuation mark (. ! ?)
have a subject which tells who or what the sentence is about
have a predicate which tells us something about the subject
(*Learning Grammar Through Writing,* pp. 28-32.)

the Poppers (subject)

felt very proud and happy (predicate)

Day 3 C.   Reason 1 - Next, Then, Naturally
Reason 2 - Sunday
Reason 3 - Stillwater, Antarctica
Reason 4 - Morning, Chronicle, Associated Press
Reason 5 - Popper, Cook, Drake, Poppers
Reason 6 - Mr., Captain, Admiral

For additional help you can use *Learning Grammar Through Writing,*
pages 41-43, as examples of capitalization rules and have your student tell
you the rule number, such as 9i, for each word.

Day 4 A.   picture

LESSON 4

Captain Cook was not happy, however. He had suddenly ceased his gay, exploring little walks about the house, and would sit most of the day, sulking, in the refrigerator. Mr. Popper had removed all the stranger objects, leaving only the marbles and checkers, so that Captain Cook now had a nice, orderly little rookery...

"Better leave him alone, children," said Mrs. Popper. "He feels mopey, I guess."

From *Mr. Popper's Penguins* by Richard and Florence Atwater. Copyright ©1938 by Florence Atwater and Richard Atwater; © renewed 1966 by Florence Atwater, Doris Atwater, and Carroll Atwater Bishop. By permission of Little, Brown and Company.

DAY 1

A. Read the passage silently. Ask your teacher to help you with difficult words. When you are ready, read the passage out loud to your teacher.

B. As your teacher reads the lines in bold print out loud,* write them down. Compare your copy to the passage on this page and make any corrections. Ask your teacher to repeat the dictation passage more than once if needed.

NOTE TO THE TEACHER: Spelling lists will be made of unknown words, misspelled words from dictation, and any unknown words from the word study activities. Please do not make weekly lists of more than 5 words. Keep track of words you do not cover and add them to later lists. Keep a list of these words from week to week, noting when they are mastered. Sheets for this purpose are found in the Appendix of this book and in the Student Activity Book.

DAY 2

A. One of the main characters in our passage is a penguin. Use an encyclopedia or a book about penguins to find information about penguins. Make a list of at least five facts about them. Include basic information, such as where they live (habitat), and how they produce offspring.

*This is on the optional Dictation Tape.

B. There are many kinds of penguins. Make a list of several kinds of penguins. Which kind is your favorite? You might want to draw or trace a picture of a penguin to include with your list.

C. Find the word rook in a dictionary, in which the definition refers to a bird. Glancing down, find the word rookery. Rookery has several definitions. What do all these definitions have in common with the rook? What does the word rookery mean in our story?

DAY 3

A. Find three words in the passage that end with -ing. Underline these words.

B. When we add -ing to the end of a word we have added a suffix. Think about this picture. The base word, or word without anything added to it, is like the main house. A suffix is a letter or letters that is added to the end of the word, like an extra room on a house. The extra room adds more uses to the house. The suffix that is put on the end of the word adds another way the word can be used. Tell your teacher what the base words (main houses) are for the words you underlined.

C. To show that something is continuing to happen, we add the ending -ing. There are three ways to add -ing to a word. Look at these three rules that your teacher will write on index cards or cut from your Student Activity Book. Listen as your teacher reads them to you.

1. When you add a suffix to a word ending in silent e, drop the e before adding an ending that begins with a vowel.

    Example: make/making

2. When you add a suffix to a word ending with a short vowel and a consonant, double the final consonant before adding an ending.

    Example: hop/hopping

3. When you add a suffix to a word that has a long vowel before a consonant, or to a word with a short vowel before two consonants, just add the ending.

    Examples: mow/mowing   bend/bending

Match the examples below to the correct rule. Write the correct examples on the back of each card.

sulk – sulking   leave – leaving

swim – swimming

D. Look at these words. Tell your teacher how you would spell these words after adding -ing. Which of the three rules would apply?

spend   take   sit   explore   clap   play

On the back of the correct card, write the word with -ing added.

DAY 4

A. Adjectives are words that tell something about nouns and pronouns. Adjectives describe nouns and pronouns by telling what kind, which one, or how many.

Two things are nicely described in our episode: the "walks" and the "rookery." Find the words that describe "walks" and "rookery," and point them out to your teacher. These words are adjectives, because they tell about Captain Cook's walks and his rookery.

B. Think of all the words you can which describe penguins, such as short, curious, awkward, etc.

C. Imagine you have a pet penguin and he is walking around your living room while you watch him. Compose several sentences describing what your penguin does and how he looks as he walks around. Use the words you listed in B, above.

DAY 5

A. Listen as your teacher reads the passage you are to write from dictation.* Do not write as it is read the first time. Just listen. Remember, writing from dictation is a skill you acquire with practice, like hitting a baseball. Your first attempts may not be too successful, but as you practice you will become better.

B. After you listen to the passage the second time, write what you have heard. When you have finished, compare your copy to the model.

C. Listen as your teacher dictates the spelling words you have been working on this

*This is on the optional Dictation Tape.

week. Write each word as she reads it to you. After you write each word, use it in a sentence orally. When you are finished, compare your spellings to the correct spellings on your list, and make any needed corrections.

NOTE TO THE TEACHER: Be sure to add correctly spelled words to a master list that you keep for each student. Record the date the words are correctly spelled.

Teacher Helps:

Day 2 C.   The rook is a social bird that lives in a large community of rooks. From this, rookery takes on the meaning of any bird that lives in communities with its own kind. This can also be applied to mammals, people living in tenements, or even to any group of animals which lives in a community of its own kind. Furthermore, rookery might refer to the place where such communities are found.

Day 3 A.   exploring, sulking, leaving

    B.   explore, sulk, leave

    C.
leave	- leaving	Rule #1
swim	- swimming	Rule #2
sulk	- sulking	Rule #3

    D.   spending (3), taking (1), sitting (2), exploring (1), clapping (2), playing (3)

Day 4 A.   gay, exploring little walks
                nice, orderly little rookery

LESSON 5

But it was soon clear that it was something worse than mopiness that ailed Captain Cook. All day he would sit with his little white-circled eyes staring out sadly from the refrigerator. His coat had lost its lovely, glossy look; his round little stomach grew flatter each day.

He would turn away now when Mrs. Popper would offer him some canned shrimps.

From *Mr. Popper's Penguins* by Richard and Florence Atwater. Copyright ©1938 by Florence Atwater and Richard Atwater; © renewed 1966 by Florence Atwater, Doris Atwater, and Carroll Atwater Bishop. By permission of Little, Brown and Company.

DAY 1

A. Read the passage silently. Ask your teacher to help you with difficult words. When you are ready, read the passage out loud to your teacher.

B. As your teacher reads the lines in bold print out loud,* write them down. Compare your copy to the passage on this page and make corrections.

NOTE TO THE TEACHER: Spelling lists will be made of unknown words, misspelled words from dictation, and any unknown words from the word study activities. Please do not make weekly lists of more than 5 words. Keep track of words you do not cover and add them to later lists. Keep a list of these words from week to week, noting when they are mastered. Sheets for this purpose are found in the Appendix of this book and in the Student Activity Book.

DAY 2

A. There was an explorer named Captain James Cook. Look up Captain James Cook in the encyclopedia, or books about explorers.

B. Make a time line (like the example), beginning with Captain James Cook's date of birth, and ending with his death. Mark each voyage on the time line with a line and the date. Make a list including the dates of his birth, his major voyages, and his death. Notice his most important achievements. For example:

*This is on the optional Dictation Tape.

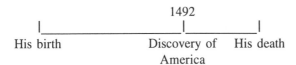

Christopher Columbus

```
                           1492
  |_____|_____|
His birth            Discovery of  His death
                      America
```

C. Why do you think Mr. Popper named the penguin Captain Cook? It is a special honor to name someone after someone else. Some children are given the same name as a relative to show honor or love for that relative. Talk with you teacher about anyone in your family who is named after a relative or friend. Who were they named after and why?

Sometimes people are not named after a relative, but after a famous person outside the family. Many people, for example, have been named after presidents. What does this tell us about how they feel about that famous person? Try to think of someone who has been named after a famous person. If you could pick someone to be named after, who would it be and why?

DAY 3 & 4

A. Reread the passage for this lesson silently. Discuss the following questions with your teacher:

1. What do you think is wrong with Captain Cook?
2. What four things in this scene show us there is something wrong with Captain Cook?
3. Tell the teacher what you think will help Captain Cook.

B. Captain Cook is like a sick friend. Talk to your teacher about ways you might help a sick friend.

A get well card is a good way to encourage a sick friend. Design a get well card for a friend or family member. On the front of your card, you might put a picture, poem, or Scripture. The best ideas will come as you think of the sick person's personal interests, like baseball or horses. Inside your card, include a greeting, a brief message, and a closing. For example:

Dear Bob,

    I am sorry that you are sick. I hope you get well soon so we can play together. I'm lonely when I don't see you for several days. Get well soon.

Your friend,

Bill

C. Review the rules for capitalizing from Lesson 3, Day 3. We will now add another rule about parts of a letter. Look at the rules on the cards your teacher shows you from Lesson 3. Copy the following new rule on an index card or cut it out of your Student Activity Book.

> Use a capital letter to begin all the words in the greeting and the first word in the closing of a letter.

Reread your letter and make sure all the words are capitalized that should be capitalized.

DAY 5

A. Listen as your teacher reads the passage you are to write from dictation.* Do not write as it is read the first time, just listen. Remember, writing from dictation is a skill you acquire with practice, like hitting a baseball. Your first attempts may not be too successful, but as you practice you will become better.

B. After you listen to the passage the second time, write what you have heard. When you have finished, compare your copy to the passage at the beginning of this lesson.

C. Listen as your teacher dictates the spelling words you have been working on this week. Write each word as she reads it to you. After you write each word, use it in a sentence orally. When you are finished, compare your spellings to the correct spellings on your list, and make any needed corrections.

NOTE TO THE TEACHER: Be sure to add correctly spelled words to a master list that you keep for each student. Record the date the words are correctly spelled.

Teacher Helps:

Day 2 B.

1728 - James Cook was born in England.	1772–1775 - 2nd voyage
1768 - 1st voyage to Pacific Ocean	1776 - 3rd voyage to Pacific
1770 - Discovered Botany Bay, Australia	1778 - Discovered Hawaii
1771 - Returned from first voyage	1779 - Died

Day 3 A. 2. All day he would sit and stare.
His coat lost its gloss.
His stomach got flatter.
He would not eat.

*This is on the optional Dictation Tape.

20

LESSON 6

That night the Poppers sat up all night, taking turns changing the ice packs.

It was no use. In the morning Mrs. Popper took Captain Cook's temperature again. It had gone up to one hundred and five.

Everyone was sympathetic. The reporter on the *Morning Chronicle* stopped in to inquire about the penguin. The neighbors brought in all sorts of broths and jellies to try to tempt the little fellow. Even Mrs. Callahan, who had never had a very high opinion of Captain Cook, made a lovely frozen custard for him. Nothing did any good. Captain Cook was too far gone.

From *Mr. Popper's Penguins* by Richard and Florence Atwater. Copyright ©1938 by Florence Atwater and Richard Atwater; © renewed 1966 by Florence Atwater, Doris Atwater, and Carroll Atwater Bishop. By permission of Little, Brown and Company.

DAY 1

A. Read the passage silently. Ask your teacher to help you with difficult words. When you are ready, read the passage out loud to your teacher.

B. As your teacher reads the lines in bold print out loud,* write them down. Compare your copy to the passage on this page and make corrections.

NOTE TO THE TEACHER: You may repeat the dictation passage more than once if needed.

Spelling lists will be made of unknown words, misspelled words from dictation, and any unknown words from the word study activities. Please do not make weekly lists of more than 5 words. Keep track of words you do not cover and add them to later lists. Keep a list of these words from week to week, noting when they are mastered. Sheets for this purpose are found in the Appendix of this book and in the Student Activity Book.

DAY 2

A. Rear Admiral Richard E. Byrd was a great Antarctic explorer. After reading about him, answer the following questions about his explorations.

1. How was Byrd's expedition different from Captain James Cook's?
2. What was the name of Byrd's base in Antarctica?

*This is on the optional Dictation Tape.

3. What was the advantage of Byrd's permanent base?
4. What was special about Operation High Jump?
5. How many years (off and on) did Byrd explore Antarctica?

B. Now that you have read about Admiral Byrd and answered the questions in Part A, look at a map of Antarctica in an Atlas or from the Appendix. In order to get familiar with the terms used when working with maps, look these words up in a dictionary, or your atlas.

longitude   latitude
key   scale

After you have read a definition for each word, tell your teacher what it means. Use your atlas to show an example for each word.

C. Using an atlas and a pencil, fill in the following locations on your map of Antarctica, found in the Appendix.

Atlantic Ocean   Pacific Ocean
Ross Sea   Antarctic Circle
Ross Ice Shelf   Weddell Sea

Label the continent with the following places:

Byrd Land   Victoria Land
Enderby Land   Wilkes Land
Queen Maud Land

After checking your locations with your teacher, carefully trace over your pencil marks with a pen or fine tip marker. Locate Antarctica on a globe as well, if available.

DAY 3

A. When the situation worsened for Captain Cook, the passage for this lesson (from *Mr. Popper's Penguins*) says that, "Everyone was sympathetic." What do you think the word sympathetic means? Don't look it up, but decide what you think by reading the rest of the passage. Tell your teacher your definition.

B. We learned in the first passage that there had been a newspaper article about Captain Cook's arrival. It seems that people were interested in how he was doing. We see that Captain Cook has many visitors, one of whom is a reporter from the local newspaper. Imagine that you are a reporter from your newspaper, and your assignment is to write about Captain Cook. Imagine that you arrive at the same time as the neighbors, and Captain Cook is surrounded by everyone handing out food and talking to him. First, write a few sentences reporting the facts from the passage. Next, write a few sentences describing how Captain Cook must feel and what he might be thinking. How would you feel if you were sick and surrounded by people holding things out, but you didn't know what they were saying?

C. Check to make sure you have answered the 5 "W" questions that are used in reporting: Who? What? When? Where? Why?

DAY 4

A. A noun is called a plural noun if what the noun names is more than one. There are quite a few plural nouns in this lesson. Circle all the plural nouns you can find.

B. Most nouns form plurals by just adding "s." However, one of the plural nouns in our lesson is different. Which one is different? How did "jelly" change from one to more than one?

C. Not all words that end in "y" change "y" to "i" and add "es." Only when there is a consonant before the "y" do we need to change it. When there is a vowel before the "y," you just add "s" to make it plural. For example, the plural of monkey is monkeys.

How would you make the following nouns plural?

penguin	day	bully	turkey	city
guy	captain	chair	spy	

DAY 5

A. Listen as your teacher reads the passage you are to write from dictation.* Do not write as it is read the first time. Just listen. Remember, writing from dictation is a skill you acquire with practice, like hitting a baseball. Your first attempts may not be too successful, but as you practice you will become better at it.

B. After you listen to the passage the second time, write what you have heard. When you have finished, compare your copy to the passage at the beginning of this lesson.

C. Listen as your teacher dictates the spelling words you have been working on this week. Write each word as she reads it to you. After you write each word, use it in

*This is on the optional Dictation Tape.

a sentence orally. When you are finished, compare your spellings to the correct spellings on your list, and make any needed corrections.

NOTE TO THE TEACHER: Be sure to add correctly spelled words to a master list that you keep for each student. Record the date the words are correctly spelled.

Teacher Helps:

Day 2 A.
1. Byrd established a permanent base in Antarctica.
2. Little America
3. He had a permanent place from which to make extended explorations and scientific studies.
4. It was the largest Antarctic expedition in history, with the help of the U.S. Navy.
5. About 28 years.

C.

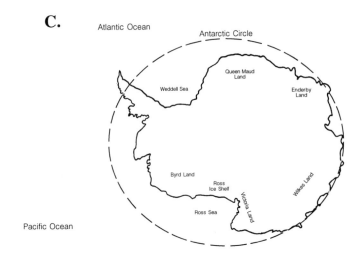

Day 3 A. In this context, "sympathetic" means that all the people felt badly about Captain Cook's condition. They expressed their feelings by trying to help.

Day 4 A. Poppers, turns, packs, neighbors, sorts, broths, jellies.

B. jellies is different
Changed "y" to "i" and added "es."

C. penguins, days, bullies, turkeys, cities
guys, captains, chairs, spies

LESSON 7

Surely if anyone anywhere had any idea what could cure a dying penguin, this man would.

Two days later there was an answer from the Curator... "Perhaps you do not know that we too have, in our aquarium at Mammoth City, a penguin from the Antarctic. It is failing rapidly, in spite of everything we have done for it. **I have wondered lately whether it is not suffering from loneliness. Perhaps that is what ails your Captain Cook. I am, therefore, shipping you, under separate cover, our penguin.** You may keep her."

And that is how Greta came to live at 432 Proudfoot Avenue.

From *Mr. Popper's Penguins* by Richard and Florence Atwater. Copyright ©1938 by Florence Atwater and Richard Atwater; © renewed 1966 by Florence Atwater, Doris Atwater, and Carroll Atwater Bishop. By permission of Little, Brown and Company.

DAY 1

A. Read the passage silently. Ask your teacher to help you with difficult words. When you are ready, read the passage out loud to your teacher.

B. As your teacher reads the lines in bold print out loud,* write them down. Compare your copy to the passage on this page and make corrections.

NOTE TO THE TEACHER: You may repeat the dictation passage more than once if needed.

Spelling lists will be made of unknown words, misspelled words from dictation, and any unknown words from the word study activities. Please do not make weekly lists of more than 5 words. Keep track of words you do not cover and add them to later lists. Keep a list of these words from week to week, noting when they are mastered. Sheets for this purpose are found in the Appendix of this book and in the Student Activity Book.

DAY 2

Your teacher will show you five simple drawings (found in the Appendix), one that represents each passage you have read in Lessons 3–7. Match each picture to the pas-

*This is on the optional Dictation Tape.

sage it represents. (Remember, all the details of the passage will not be in the picture, so look for the most important idea, or main idea from each passage.) Put the five pictures in the correct order in which they happened in the story.

A. The passages we have read from *Mr. Popper's Penguins* are written as narrative because they tell us the events of a story. When you tell the events of a story, you are narrating. Narrating is a good way to remember the events and details of a story.

B. After putting the pictures in order, retell the story of Captain Cook and the Poppers as it was told in the passages.

C. Using both the passages and the pictures, talk with your teacher and make up one sentence that tells the main idea of each passage. Write it on the back of each picture.

DAY 3 & 4

For the past few weeks, we have been accumulating information about penguins, Antarctica, and explorers to Antarctica. We now have enough information to write a report.

A written report is organized so that your thoughts are in order. When your thoughts are in order they are easy to understand. The thoughts for your report are made into sentences. The sentences are made into paragraphs. Finally, the paragraphs are made into a report.

You have already written many sentences for your research assignment each week. Now it is time to make these sentences into paragraphs. A paragraph is a group of sentences about one main thing, called a topic. So far, your topics have been Antarctica, penguins, Admiral Byrd, and Captain James Cook. When we write a paragraph, our first sentence tells the topic. This sentence is called the "topic sentence." The rest of the sentences must tell us something about the topic.

NOTE TO THE TEACHER: At this point, it might be confusing to introduce the subject of paragraph coherence. If your child relates the sentences in his paragraph to one topic, he will have achieved enough coherence for this age level.

For example, one of your topics is penguins. You might have some sentences about penguins that look like this:

Penguins are birds.
They have wings, but they don't fly.

Penguins lay eggs in their nests.
Some different kinds of penguins are emperor, king, and macaroni.
Penguins live in the water, but they make nests on land.

We know that the topic for all our sentences is the penguin, but we need a topic sentence. A good topic sentence might be "Penguins are birds." All the other sentences are about this topic. A good order, but not the only order for these sentences, might be like this:

Penguins are birds. They have wings, but they don't fly. Penguins live in the water, but they make nests on land. Penguins lay eggs in their nests. Some different kinds of penguins are emperor, king, and macaroni.

Write one paragraph about Antarctica and one about penguins. Include about five or six sentences per paragraph. Use the notes from the research which you did in previous lessons.

DAY 5

You have done a great deal of work gathering information and learning about the Antarctic, explorers, and penguins. Now that you have finished writing a report, you should be very pleased with yourself. Share your report with your family or friends by reading it to them, and showing them any pictures you have drawn or the books you have used to help you. You can also present your report to others by telling them what is in the report instead of reading it to them.

It may seem hard to present reports orally at first. The more you practice, the easier it will become.

Teacher Helps:

Day 2
1. Front page of Morning Chronicle.
2. Close-up of Captain Cook sulking.
3. Captain Cook refusing the canned shrimp.
4. Poppers, neighbors, and reporter, etc.
5. Crate at door from Mammoth City Aquarium.

LESSON 8

DAY 1

Does your mother, father or teacher read aloud to you? Talk to your teacher about the things you like and don't like about being read to by someone.

This week you are going to prepare a read-aloud presentation for your family, class, or teacher.

The first step is to choose the story, poem, or scripture passage that you will present. Before choosing your passage, consider who your audience will be for the presentation. A group of children may enjoy a funny poem. Grandparents may prefer a story or scripture passage. With your teacher, decide who your audience will be and then begin looking for your presentation material.

DAY 2

Read the material (story, poem, or scripture) you have chosen in Day 1 to understand the meaning of it. Talk to your teacher about words you do not understand. Try to find out what the author wanted to communicate.

Read the material again looking for the emotion (feelings) behind the words. Did the author want us to laugh, cry, learn, etc. when we read this work? Talk to your teacher about how you might use your voice to express these feelings. Ask these questions:

1. What will I emphasize as I speak?
2. Where will I pause as I speak?
3. Will I use my voice in any other manner to communicate the meaning?

If you will be presenting a story, you may need to use a different voice for each character.

DAYS 3 & 4

Practice reading your material aloud at least three times each day. You are not required to memorize the entire passage, however, you should know it well enough to be able to look up from your book several times during the presentation.

Stand in front of a mirror as you practice. Use the following list to help you evaluate yourself. After you have practiced several times, ask your teacher or another student to evaluate you, using the list.

_____ 1. Do I read slowly?
_____ 2. Do I read clearly?
_____ 3. Do I read loud enough?
_____ 4. Am I using my voice well to communicate the meaning and feeling?
_____ 5. Am I standing up straight, but naturally?
_____ 6. Do I look at my audience enough?

DAY 5

Your presentation day has arrived, and even though you may feel nervous, you are ready for your audience because you planned for it. If you feel very nervous, ask your teacher to sit in the back of the room and give you support by smiling at you.

LESSON 9

DAY 1

A. Listen as your teacher reads the story *Paul Bunyan and the Whistlin' River* found in the Appendix.* Try to enjoy the type of language used to tell the story.

B. After listening, tell your teacher the answer to these questions:

    1. What is the problem, or conflict, that starts the story?
    2. How would you describe the Whistlin' River?
    3. How would you describe Paul Bunyan?
    4. How did Paul "straighten out" his problem?

C. The events of a story are called the plot. Choose one aspect of the plot to illustrate, such as the Whistlin' River standing up, or Paul and Babe capturing the blizzards. If you do not choose to draw a picture, write a paragraph describing what you would draw. Tell how your picture would look.

DAY 2

A. Read the story *Paul Bunyan and the Whistlin' River* silently. Retell the story to your teacher.

B. Find each of these words in your story. Read the sentence that contains each word aloud to your teacher. Using the story to help you, tell your teacher what you think each word means. If you can't come up with a definition, look up each word in the dictionary.

        gumption   persnickety
        ornery

C. Make up a new sentence using each word. Write each sentence and then use a thesaurus or dictionary to help you think of another word that is close in meaning to each of your words. Read your sentences, replacing the words with the synonyms.

DAY 3

A. Our story, *Paul Bunyan and the Whistlin' River* is an example of a tall tale.

*This is on the optional Dictation Tape.

30

Tall tales are a very important part of America's folk tradition. That is, they originated as simple stories told, and retold, by common people—sometimes about real "heroes," and sometimes not—but always about things, situations or occupations that were well-known to the listeners. Characteristics found in just about all tall tales include humor, exaggeration, larger-than-life heroes, and use of phrases, words and dialects common to the areas where the stories originated.

Each region of the country gave birth to its own set of tall tales: the eastern seaboard had Captain Stormalong and his great ship, the *Courser*; railroad workers sang about the mighty Casey Jones; the south and mid-west celebrated John Henry and Mike Fink; and the west spun wild yarns about Pecos Bill and Davy Crockett. Of course, these are only a few of the many heroic legends made famous through tall tales, because America's folk tradition is as rich and varied as the country itself.

You may want to check the library for books or videos on tall tales.

B. Look over your story and find three or four examples of exaggeration and point them out to your teacher. One example is the description of the river squirting him with 4,287 gallons of water. That's a lot of water. Also talk with your teacher about what point you think the author is trying to make by using exaggeration in each case.

C. Talking with your teacher, come up with exaggerated descriptions to complete these phrases:

> The tree was so tall it _____.
> The noise was as loud as _____.

If you have any other tall tales that you can read, try to find more examples of exaggeration.

DAY 4

A. Yesterday, we looked at the element of exaggeration in tall tales. Another common element of tall tales is that the hero or heroine is larger-than-life. Another way to describe the main character is super human. Make a list of several of the things that Paul Bunyan does in our story that are larger-than-life.

B. The heroes or heroines of tall tales usually demonstrate qualities such as braveness, strength and cleverness. Tell your teacher how Paul Bunyan showed his strength. How did he show his cleverness?

C. The hero/heroine of a tall tale always has a big problem to solve, or a strong foe to defeat. Tell about the force that opposes Paul in our story. Do you think this foe would defeat a normal man?

DAY 5

A. Another common element of a tall tale is humor. If you have exaggeration, you are bound to have humor. The idea of someone eating two boxcars full of pancakes, or stacking bunkhouses can be pretty funny. Look over your story and find at least two examples of humor. List these examples on your paper and discuss them with your teacher.

B. Humor can be expressed in different ways. We can read something that is funny, we can say something humorous, or we can do something that brings a smile to our lips. Pretend you are Paul Bunyan. Act out some or all of the parts of the story for your family. You may want to dress like you think Paul Bunyan might have dressed. While you act the story out, also tell the story from Paul Bunyan's point of view. For example, tell about when the river squirted you in the face and what you did about it.

C. Often, the end of a tall tale will provide a new explanation for why something is the way it is. What happens to the forests in Texas at the end of our story?

Teacher Helps:

Day 1 B.
    1. The river squirts Paul Bunyan twice with water.
    2. ornery, trouble-causing, playful
    3. big, strong, upset, poetic
    4. By making the Whistlin' River freeze, hooking it up to Babe with logging chains and pulling it straight.

Day 2 B.
    gumption - courage; nerve; initiative
    persnickety - opinionated
    ornery - obstinate; having an ugly disposition

Day 3 B. ...203 feet tall...

...could be heard 679 miles in every direction.

...squirted 4,287 gallons of water...

..a light breakfast of 2 boxcars of sourdough pancakes.

...he began sawing the river into 9 mile lengths...

C. The tree was so tall it touched the sky.

The noise was as loud as a thousand airplanes.

Day 4 A. ...let out a yell that set off a considerable landslide...

...covering the distance in long strides that caused windstorms...

...tiptoed 40 or 50 miles...

B. Paul showed his strength by helping Babe pull the river straight.

Paul showed his cleverness by figuring out how to catch the blizzards.

C. Paul is opposed by the river itself.

Day 5 A. So it was regular practice for logging camps all the way up into Alaska to hire 2 or 12 men whose main job was called "whistle-listener."

...squirted 4,287 gallons of water straight into Ol' Paul's beard.

...[Paul] took care to keep pine trees and trapped eagles and boulders combed out of it [his beard] regularly.

...complete with a batch of mud turtles, 77 large carp, and 2 very confused beavers.

C. Thanks to Paul Bunyan delivering sections of the Whistlin' River to logging camps, the forests of Texas became a productive logging industry.

LESSONS 10 & 11

DAYS 1-10

For the next two weeks, you are going to write your own tall tale. Take your time and enjoy your story.

We have already identified the elements of a tall tale (in Lesson 9.) They are: exaggeration, humor, and superhuman qualities of the hero or heroine. Another element of a tall tale is the language or dialect common to the area in which the story takes place. For example, in the West a phrase such as "Howdy, partner!" would be common. In the South, people might say "Hi, y'all." The language in a tall tale not only tells where the story takes place, it is also a reflection of the "color" and style of that area.

Step 1 - Think About Your Story

As you begin to think about the story you want to write, talk to your teacher about these things:

1. the location of your story
2. a hero or heroine
3. what problem your hero / heroine will face
4. equipping your hero / heroine with larger than life abilities
5. the exaggeration and humor you will use in your story
6. the conversation, or dialogue you will use in your story
7. colorful descriptions and sayings that your hero / heroine can use

Step 2 - Brainstorming

Use the Tall Tale Chart found in the Appendix or your Student Activity Book to make notes for your story. You or your teacher can fill out the chart as you talk about your story. Describe your hero/heroine, including superhuman qualities & exaggeration. Remember, the setting can determine the dialect used in your story. Be sure to use a pencil as you brainstorm because you will probably change your mind as you talk about the story.

Step 3 - Make A List

Your story will include several events. Think about these events and talk to your teacher about them. On a blank sheet of paper, make a list of events that will occur in your story. You should write events that will bring about the problem that you wrote in the "Problem" box of your Tall Tale chart, and that will bring about the solution that you wrote in the "Solution" box of your Tall Tale Chart. Use words or phrases. Be sure to number your list in the order the events will happen in the story.

Once you have decided on the characters and events of your story, you may begin drawing illustrations for each event. Draw each illustration on a separate sheet of white paper.

Step 4 - Begin Writing

You will need one piece of notebook paper for each event in the Problem section of your story. Use the first piece of paper for your first event. Begin writing 1/3 of the way down on your paper. Write two or three sentences describing the event, writing on every other line. Do the same for each of your other events.

Step 5 - Write Topic Sentences

Each paragraph in your story will begin with a "topic sentence." Reread one of your pages from Step 4, describing an event in your story. What is the most important thing you want your reader to know about this event? Talk to your teacher about this most important thing.

On the top of your sheet, above the other sentences, write a sentence describing this most important thing. This is your topic sentence for the paragraph about this event.

Repeat this procedure for each event in your story. When you have completed this step, you will have written a paragraph for each event in your story.

Step 6 - Edit Your Paragraph

Reread each one of your paragraphs. As you read, ask yourself these questions:

* Can I describe a scene or person more fully?
* Can I use figurative language in this paragraph? (For example: He was as mad as a bear with a toothache.)
* Can I include dialect in this paragraph?
* Can I add exaggeration or humor in this event?

Step 7 - Write An Introduction For Your Tall Tale

Read the first paragraph from our example *Paul Bunyan and the Whistlin' River,* (found in the Appendix – Lesson 9). The first paragraph of a story is called the introduction. Your introduction should help your readers get acquainted with the places and people in your story. Don't give away what the ending will be.

Step 8 - Write A Conclusion For Your Story

Bring the events and struggles to a close for your hero or heroine. Remember, in tall tales, most heroes succeed in the end. Decide whether or not you want your hero to prevail. Use your imagination to make up a great ending.

Step 9 - Make A Final Copy Of Your Story

Rewrite or type your story, complete with the Title, and the name of the Author (you!). Start with the Introduction, then include the "Problem" events and the "Solution" events in the order in which you determined they should occur. Lastly, write out your conclusion. Read your tall tale to yourself and enjoy it.

Step 10 - Present Your Tall Tale

Read your story to family or friends, or ask your teacher to read the story while you act it out. Illustrations make a nice addition to your story, so be sure to show your audience the illustrations you drew for each event (in Step 3.) Put your story and illustrations in a folder, or staple them inside two pieces of construction paper for a cover. You'll want to share your tall tale with others in the years to come.

LESSON 12

The Trumpet of the Swan
by E.B. White

"Well," said the cob, "I guess it's no use. I guess you are dumb."

When he heard the word "dumb," Louis felt like crying. The cob saw that he had hurt Louis' feelings. "You misunderstand me, my son," he said in a comforting voice. "You failed to understand my use of the word 'dumb,' which has two meanings. If I had called you a dumb cluck or a dumb bunny, that would have meant that I had a poor opinion of your intelligence. Actually, I think you are perhaps the brightest, smartest, most intelligent of all my cygnets. Words sometimes have two meanings; the word 'dumb' is such a word. ...A person who can't speak is called dumb. That simply means he can't say anything. Do you understand?"

The Trumpet of the Swan by E.B. White. Text ©1970 by E.B. White.
Selection reprinted by permission of HarperCollins Publishers.

DAY 1

A. Listen to your teacher read the passage.* Read the passage silently. Ask your teacher to help you with difficult words. When you are ready, read the passage out loud to your teacher. In your own words, tell your teacher what is happening in this passage.

B. As your teacher reads the lines in bold print out loud,* write them down. Compare your copy to the passage on this page and make corrections.

NOTE TO THE TEACHER: Spelling lists will be made of unknown words, misspelled words from dictation, and any unknown words from the word study activities. Please do not make weekly lists of more than 5 words. Keep track of words you do not cover and add them to later lists. Keep a list of these words from week to week, noting when they are mastered. Sheets for this purpose are found in the Appendix of this book and in the Student Activity Book.

*Due to publisher's restrictions, passages from *The Trumpet of the Swan* are not included on the Dictation Tape.

DAY 2

A. Our passage provides part of an imagined conversation between a father swan (called a cob) and his son (a cygnet). The cygnet, named Louis, has a problem. Talk with your teacher about the limitation that Louis has and what we call his problem.

B. In the story, Louis' problem is called a <u>conflict</u>. This is the main problem that causes the action during the rest of the story. During the next few passages, look for solutions or answers for Louis' conflict.

C. Together with your teacher, make a list of 2 or 3 possible problems that might be faced by a swan without a voice. What kind of problems might be faced by a person who can't speak? Make a list of 4 or 5 of the possible problems of the person who can't speak. Do you think a person who can't speak likes to be called, dumb? Do you think they would prefer to be called mute? Look up the word "mute" and tell your teacher what you think.

DAY 3

A. We have identified the problem Louis is having—he can't speak, or more specifically, he can't make the noises that swans make. Louis is a trumpeter swan, which is a white swan that lives in North America, and is known for its loud and impressive call. You may want to look for more information on trumpeter swans in an encyclopedia or book on swans.

B. Louis can't speak, and that makes it difficult for him to make himself understood. When his father said he was dumb, Louis misunderstood. Misunderstandings can cause people's feelings to be hurt. Have you ever misunderstood someone? How did you feel? Talk with your teacher about good ways to correct misunderstandings. Can you think of ways to avoid misunderstandings?

C. Louis misunderstood because his father used a homonym. His father has given us a definition of homonyms, or words that sound the same and are spelled the same but have two different meanings. Tell your teacher the homonym that was used and explain the two meanings. Use a dictionary to look up the meanings of these homonyms:

beach	track	charge
drive	slip	last

Make sure to use these words carefully so you won't be misunderstood!

DAY 4

A. Louis wrongly understood what his father meant. Look at the word "misunderstand," and tell how you think the meaning of the word "understand" was changed to make the word "misunderstand." Was something added?

B. A letter, or letters added to the front of a word, that changes its meaning is called a <u>prefix</u>. Specific prefixes change the meanings of words in specific ways. The prefix mis- means wrongly. Look at this list of words with your teacher. Tell your teacher how you would spell them if you added the prefix mis- to each one.

spell   count   read   place

C. Prefixes are not always words by themselves, but usually make an additional syllable, or sound, when added to the base word. Think of it as a building. The base word is the original house. Prefixes are parts that are added to the front of the house that change the meaning, like a garage.

The house is larger now, and can be used for more things. So, your original word can be used in new ways because of the prefix.

Tell your teacher what each of the new words you made by adding the prefix mis- means, and then use them in a sentence orally or in writing.

DAY 5

A. Listen as your teacher reads the passage you are to write from dictation. Do not write as it is read the first time. Just listen. Remember, writing from dictation is a skill you acquire with practice, like hitting a baseball. Your first attempts may not be too successful, but as you practice you will become better.

B. After you listen to the passage the second time, write what you have heard. When you have finished, compare your copy to the passage at the beginning of this lesson.

C. Listen as your teacher dictates the spelling words you have been working on this week. Write each word as she reads it to you. After you write each word, use it in a sentence orally. When you are finished, compare your spellings to the correct spellings on your list, and make any needed corrections.

NOTE TO THE TEACHER: Be sure to add correctly spelled words to a master list that you keep for each student. Record the date the words are correctly spelled.

Teacher Helps:

Day 2 A. Louis can't speak. Not being able to speak is sometimes referred to as being "dumb."

Day 3 C. dumb - someone of poor intelligence
- someone who can't speak

Day 4 A. The letters "mis" were added.

B. misspell, miscount, misread, misplace

C. He will practice spelling words so he won't <u>misspell</u> them.
You will get a wrong answer if you <u>miscount</u>.
Look at the letters carefully so you won't <u>misread</u> them.
Did he <u>misplace</u> the map?

LESSON 13

"Do not let an unnatural sadness settle over you, Louis," said the cob. "Swans must be cheerful, not sad; graceful, not awkward; brave, not cowardly. **Remember that the world is full of youngsters who have some sort of handicap that they must overcome.** *You* **apparently have a speech defect. I am sure you will overcome it, in time.** There may even be some slight advantage, at your age, in not being able to say anything. It compels you to be a good listener. The world is full of talkers, but it is rare to find anyone who listens."

The Trumpet of the Swan by E.B. White. Text ©1970 by E.B. White.
Selection reprinted by permission of HarperCollins Publishers.

DAY 1

A. Read the passage silently. Ask your teacher to help you with difficult words. When you are ready, read the passage out loud to your teacher. In your own words, tell your teacher what is happening in this passage.

B. As your teacher reads the lines in bold print out loud, write them down. Compare your copy to the passage on this page and make corrections.

NOTE TO THE TEACHER: Spelling lists will be made of unknown words, misspelled words from dictation, and any unknown words from the word study activities. Please do not make weekly lists of more than 5 words. Keep track of words you do not cover and add them to later lists. Keep a list of these words from week to week, noting when they are mastered. Sheets for this purpose are found in the Appendix of this book and in the Student Activity Book.

DAY 2

A. We learned in the first passage that Louis has a problem. Do you remember that problem? This problem is described two ways in the passage. Find the descriptions and point them out to your teacher.

B. As the passage says, many people have handicaps that they must overcome. Talk with your teacher about the following conditions that are considered handicaps, and the ways people overcome them or continue their lives in spite of them.

deafness   blindness   physical limitations

C. Helen Keller was a famous American woman who overcame many handicaps. Look her up in an encyclopedia. After reading about Helen Keller, tell your teacher what her handicaps were and how she overcame the obstacles she faced. Do you think Helen Keller's life was inspiring? Make a list of three ways her life inspires you.

If you would like to know more about Helen Keller, go to the library and check out a book about her life. Her famous autobiography (a book she wrote about herself) is called *The Story of My Life*.

DAY 3

A. In the second sentence of our passage there are three pairs of words that are opposites, or antonyms. The way these words are used in this sentence show comparisons between one thing and another. Underline the word pairs in the second sentence that are opposites.

B. The last two sentences of our passage also have a pair of words that are opposites. Find this word pair and underline them. Why do you think the cob is using words that are opposites? Do you think it will help Louis understand?

C. Rewrite the advice given in this passage in your own words. Encourage Louis with the same ideas that his father has used, but don't use the same words. Talk about your ideas with your teacher before you write.

DAY 4

A. When an ending is added to a word, it changes the meaning of the word. Remember the picture we used to show base words? The main house is the base word, and the extra room on the right is a suffix. Here's an example:

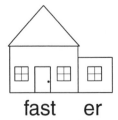

fast   er

Find the words in the passage with the ending -ful added to them and circle them.

How many syllables, or sounds, does the suffix -ful add to each word?

B. The two "-ful" words in our passage are cheerful and graceful. What do you think the suffix -ful means? Tell your teacher what you think these words mean. If you are unsure, look them up in the dictionary. Read this list of words to your teacher and tell her what you think they mean.

playful   beautiful   careful

C. Look at these words and tell your teacher when changes need to be made in a base word to add -ful.

arm - armful   care - careful
beauty - beautiful   play - playful

When do changes need to be made, and what changes do you make?

Add the suffix -ful to these words and write a sentence using each one.

color   joy   bounty

DAY 5

A. Listen as your teacher reads the passage you are to write from dictation. Do not write as it is read the first time. Just listen. Remember, writing from dictation is a skill you acquire with practice, like hitting a baseball. Your first attempts may not be too successful, but as you practice you will become better.

B. After you listen to the passage the second time, write what you have heard. When you have finished, compare your copy to the passage at the beginning of this lesson.

C. Listen as your teacher dictates the spelling words you have been working on this week. Write each word as she reads it to you. After you write each word, use it in a sentence orally. When you are finished, compare your spellings to the correct spellings on your list, and make any needed corrections.

NOTE TO THE TEACHER: Be sure to add correctly spelled words to a master list that you keep for each student. Record the date the words are correctly spelled.

Teacher Helps:

Day 2 A.   He can't make any sounds—he is unable to speak.
handicap, speech defect

Day 3 A.   cheerful – sad, graceful – awkward, brave – cowardly

     B.   listener – talker

Day 4 A.   cheerful, graceful. The suffix -ful adds one syllable.

     C.   When the base word ends in a consonant and "y," drop the "y" before adding the suffix -ful.

        colorful, joyful, bountiful

LESSON 14

"There are mechanical devices that convert air into beautiful sounds. One such device is called a trumpet. I saw a trumpet once, in my travels. **I think you may need a trumpet in order to live a full life. I've _never known_ a Trumpeter Swan to need a trumpet, but your case is different. I intend to get you what you need.** I don't know how I will manage this, but in the fullness of time it shall be accomplished. And now that our talk has come to a close, let us return gracefully to the other end of the pond, where your mother and your brothers and sisters await us!"

The Trumpet of the Swan by E.B. White. Text ©1970 by E.B. White. Selection reprinted by permission of HarperCollins Publishers.

DAY 1

A. Read the passage silently. Ask your teacher to help you with difficult words. When you are ready, read the passage out loud to your teacher. In your own words, tell your teacher what is happening in this passage.

B. As your teacher reads the lines in bold print out loud, write them down. Compare your copy to the passage on this page and make corrections.

NOTE TO THE TEACHER: Spelling lists will be made of unknown words, misspelled words from dictation, and any unknown words from the word study activities. Please do not make weekly lists of more than 5 words. Keep track of words you do not cover and add them to later lists. Keep a list of these words from week to week, noting when they are mastered. Sheets for this purpose are found in the Appendix of this book and in the Student Activity Book.

DAY 2

A. In our passage we have examples of adjectives (describing words) and adverbs (words that tell us how something was done, or when, or where or how much.) Adverbs often end in the letters -ly. Find the adverb in your passage that ends with -ly. What does this adverb tell us about the swans?

45

B. Copy this list of words and add -ly to the end of each. Read the new list to your teacher and make up an oral sentence using each word.

quick	sad	bright
slow	loud	brave

C. Look back at the first passage we used from *The Trumpet of the Swan* in Lesson 10. Find the two words in the passage that end in -ly. Write them down, and look up their definitions in the dictionary. Notice that the part of speech is listed right after the phonetic spelling. What part of speech is listed for these words? Tell your teacher what these words mean after reading their definitions, and explain how they help you understand our passage.

DAY 3

A. In our passage, there are several words which look the same, and are pronounced the same, but have more than one meaning. These words are called homonyms. One of these words is "case" which can mean "a situation," or "a carton." Can you find another word which has two meanings? Tell your teacher at least two definitions for the word you find. Use a dictionary if necessary.

B. Make up a sentence orally using "order" or "saw" for each of the definitions you have given for these words. How do you know which definition is being used in our passage? The context, or other sentences help us know which meaning is being used.

C. Tell your teacher the meanings you know for the following words. Make up an oral sentence for all meanings of each word. You may use a dictionary if needed.

safe	hit	bat
base	bag	run

Can you tell the common theme of these words? Each of these words have other meanings based on the context in which they are used—so always read carefully!

DAY 4

A. The cob has brought a problem to his son's attention. Louis probably wasn't very aware of his differences from the other cygnets, but now he is more aware. This will probably make Louis feel uncomfortable, but may be the beginning of learning how to cope with problems. Talk with your parent about problems that you have been made aware of about yourself, or a problem they were made aware of as children. How did they deal with their problems? How have you tried to cope with differences you might feel?

B. Part of helping with a problem is making the person aware of it. Another part is helping the person find a way to solve the problem. Tell your teacher how Louis' father plans to help Louis.

C. Talk with your teacher about specific ways to help people with problems such as blindness, deafness or physical impairments. There are devices that have been designed especially to help these people do things that would otherwise be hard.

It used to be thought that people were born with physical or mental limitations as a punishment from God toward the parents. As a result, people often hid family members who were handicapped. Do you think people who are handicapped are being punished by God? Talk with your parents about what you believe.

Realizing that everyone has some sort of obstacle to overcome, think about the meaning of these Scriptures and how you can apply them when relating to people with limitations.

John 9:1-3   Psalm 139:14-16

DAY 5

A. Listen as your teacher reads the passage you are to write from dictation. Do not write as it is read the first time, just listen. Remember, writing from dictation is a skill you acquire with practice, like hitting a baseball. Your first attempts may not be too successful, but as you practice you will become better.

B. After you listen to the passage the second time, write what you have heard. When you have finished, compare your copy to the passage at the beginning of this lesson.

C. Listen as your teacher dictates the spelling words you have been working on this week. Write each word as she reads it to you. After you write each word, use it in a sentence orally. When you are finished, compare your spellings to the correct spellings on your list, and make any needed corrections.

NOTE TO THE TEACHER: Be sure to add correctly spelled words to a master list that you keep for each student. Record the date the words are correctly spelled.

Teacher Helps:

Day 2 A. *Learning Grammar Through Writing,* 3a & 3g.
gracefully
It tells how the swans swam.

    C. actually, simply
adverb

Day 3 A. order - a command / harmony / sequence

          saw - past tense of see / tool for cutting wood

    C. baseball

LESSON 15

The cob turned and swam off. Louis followed. It had been an unhappy morning for him. He felt frightened at being different from his brothers and sisters. It scared him to be different. He couldn't understand why he had come into the world without a voice. Everyone else seemed to have a voice. Why didn't he? "Fate is cruel," he thought. "Fate is cruel to me." Then he remembered that his father had promised to help, and he felt better.

The Trumpet of the Swan by E.B. White. Text ©1970 by E.B. White.
Selection reprinted by permission of HarperCollins Publishers.

DAY 1

A. Read the passage silently. Ask your teacher to help you with difficult words. When you are ready, read the passage out loud to your teacher. In your own words, tell your teacher what is happening in this passage.

B. As your teacher reads the lines in bold print out loud, write them down. Compare your copy to the passage on this page and make corrections.

NOTE TO THE TEACHER: Spelling lists will be made of unknown words, misspelled words from dictation, and any unknown words from the word study activities. Please do not make weekly lists of more than 5 words. Keep track of words you do not cover and add them to later lists. Keep a list of these words from week to week, noting when they are mastered. Sheets for this purpose are found in the Appendix of this book and in the Student Activity Book.

DAY 2

A. Look at your passage and underline each word in the passage that ends with -ed. Many action words (verbs) show that something has already happened by adding the suffix -ed. Review the rules given in Lesson 4, Day 3 C. for adding a suffix to a word. The same rules apply to adding the suffix -ed.

NOTE TO THE TEACHER: The verbs "frightened" and "remembered" do not follow any of the rules as listed in Lesson 4, Day 3 C. In actuality, these words adhere to what could be called the "Extended Version" of Rule 1. This "Extended Rule 1" states that the final consonant is not doubled if the final syllable of the base word is unaccented. Since we are not teaching the Extended Version of Rule 1 at this level, we suggest that you remove the words "frightened" and "remembered" from your student's list (as written in this Activity) before proceeding with the rest of this Activity.

Tell your teacher which rule (1, 2, or 3) applies to each of the words ending with -ed that you underlined.

B. Some action words (verbs) show that something has already happened without adding the suffix -ed. Find the words that tell us that the following action words have already happened. Circle them in the passage.

Swim - Today I swim, yesterday I _____.
Think - Today I think, yesterday I _____.
Feel - Today I feel, yesterday I _____.

C. We will look at groups of verbs that do not use the suffix -ed to show that something has already happened. These are called irregular verbs because they do not follow the regular pattern. The first group of irregular verbs has a secret connection—see if you can guess what it is. Make a list of the irregular verbs and their past tense. If you do not know what the past tense is, look the word up in the dictionary.

1.   bring _____.
2.   catch _____.
3.   fight _____.
4.   seek _____.
5.   teach _____.
6.   think _____.

DAY 3

A. Louis feels afraid because he now realizes how different he is from the other cygnets. Do you think that this is an understandable feeling for Louis? Can you think of any situations where you felt very different from everyone else? What did you do? Did it change the way you acted? Talk with your teacher about that situation.

B. Ask your parents if they have ever had to deal with feeling very different from everyone else. Ask them how they handled the situation, and what advice they would give you to keep in mind if you have to face a similar situation. The comfort and advice of a parent is very important when you face a trying situation. Read the last line of our passage. Tell how Louis felt about his father's promise.

C. Look back at each one of our passages from *The Trumpet of the Swan*. Each passage contains statements from Louis' father that tells what he thinks of Louis and what he will do to help him. Write a friendly letter to Louis and tell him what his father thinks of him, and how he will help. If you do not remember the proper form of a friendly letter, ask your teacher to help you.

DAY 4

A. In our passage, Louis talks about something called fate. Look this word up in the dictionary and tell your teacher the definition. If you do not know what the word cruel means, look that up too. Combining the two definitions, tell what you think Louis means by the statement "Fate is cruel to me."

B. Do you believe that fate controls your life? Talk with your parents about your answer, and ask them what they believe. Why do you think Louis believes that fate caused him not to have a voice?

C. Listen as your teacher reads Psalm 139:14-16. The author of this psalm is David. Do you think David believes that fate is controlling his life? Who does David believe has ordained his days?

DAY 5

A. Listen as your teacher reads the passage you are to write from dictation. Do not write as it is read the first time, just listen. Remember, writing from dictation is a skill you acquire with practice, like hitting a baseball. Your first attempts may not be too successful, but as you practice you will become better.

B. After you listen to the passage the second time, write what you have heard. When you have finished, compare your copy to the passage at the beginning of this lesson.

C. Listen as your teacher dictates the spelling words you have been working on this week. Write each word as she reads it to you. After you write each word, use it in a sentence orally. When you are finished, compare your spellings to the correct spellings on your list, and make any needed corrections.

NOTE TO THE TEACHER: Be sure to add correctly spelled words to a master list that you keep for each student. Record the date the words are correctly spelled.

Teacher Helps:

Day 2 A.   turned (3), scared (1), seemed (3), promised (1)

      B.   swam, thought, felt

      C.   *Learning Grammar Through Writing,* 2o

          brought, caught, fought, sought, taught, thought

Day 3 B.   The thoughts of his father helping made Louis feel better.

      C.   Date

    Dear (Person's name),

        (Write one or two paragraphs about what Louis' father thinks of him and how he will help.)

                                              Your friend,
                                              (Put your name here)

LESSON 16

America, the Beautiful
by Katherine Lee Bates (1859-1929)

O beautiful for spacious skies.
For amber waves of grain.
For purple mountain majesties
Above the fruited plain!
America! America!
God shed His grace on thee
And crown thy good with brotherhood
From sea to shining sea!

Day 1

A. Listen while your teacher reads the passage aloud.* Read the verse silently while your teacher reads it aloud a second time. As your teacher reads, listen to the descriptions and try to imagine the settings described.

B. Look over the passage and point out any words you don't know. Adjectives (describing words) are words that help paint pictures. Adjectives tell about the naming words (nouns and pronouns) that they come before. Find the adjectives that describe these nouns in our passage and underline them:

> skies   waves of grain   sea

C. Use your dictionary and look up the adjectives you found Activity B above. After reading the definitions, tell your teacher in your own words what you think each adjective means. Make up another sentence orally using each of the adjectives.

DAY 2

A. Punctuation helps us understand what words and phrases mean. Punctuation marks (such as commas and exclamation points) also help us read correctly. Listen as your teacher reviews the rules for reading an exclamation point and comma.

  a) A sentence that ends with an exclamation point is read with strong emotion.
  b) When reading a sentence aloud that contains commas, pause when you come to the comma.

*This is on the optional Dictation Tape.

B. Using a yellow pencil, circle the commas in our passage. Like a yellow light in traffic, yellow circles remind us to pause when we are reading aloud, but not to stop completely. Using a red pencil, circle the exclamation points.

C. Since you have heard the passage read, learned the meaning of the words, and studied the punctuation, you are now ready to begin reading the passage with expression. Practice reading the passage as if you were presenting it for others. Speak slowly and clearly, with a voice loud enough to be easily heard. You may want to tape record yourself reading the passage so that you can make improvements. Begin memorizing the passage as well.

DAY 3

A. The title of our passage is *America, the Beautiful*. This is a good description of our country. Either by looking through magazines, newspapers, catalogs, travel brochures or your family's own photographs, choose four pictures that show some part of *America the Beautiful*. Mount or glue the pictures on construction paper or in the Student Activity Book. (Ask your teacher for permission before cutting them out.)

B. In this lesson, Day 1, we looked at the adjectives the author used in our passage to describe America. Make a list of three or four words that describe each picture. For example, looking at a picture of a mountain sunset, one might use these adjectives to describe it: colorful, grand, peaceful, beautiful.

C. Write one or two sentences that describe each picture using the adjectives on your list.

DAY 4

Listen as your teacher reads the passage about *America, the Beautiful* from *Color the Patriotic Classics* found in the Appendix.* You may want to color the picture of the 1893 Chicago World's Fair, attended by the woman who wrote *America, the Beautiful*, Katharine Lee Bates.

DAY 5

A. Our passage contains eight lines, with two parts containing four lines each. Read the first four lines and tell your teacher what you think the author is telling you about America. What do the last four lines sound like to you?

*This is on the optional Dictation Tape.

B. In our passage at the beginning of the lesson, *America, the Beautiful* follows a pattern. Count the number of syllables in each line, then tell your teacher the syllable pattern of the verse. Notice which words rhyme. Point them out to your teacher.

Using the sentences you wrote on Day 3, or something new, try to make up a four sentence poem that follows this pattern of 8 syllables, 6 syllables, 8 syllables and 6 syllables, with the last word in the 2nd and 4th lines rhyming. Illustrate your poem with your own drawings or another picture cut out of a magazine.

Example:

I'd like to climb this tree today.
It is so very tall.
I'll watch my step and hold on tight.
So I won't slip and fall.

C. Present the passage to family or friends by reading or reciting from memory. You may also want to present the poem you have written during this activity.

Teacher Helps:

Day 1 B.   *Learning Grammar Through Writing,* 3a.

spacious skies, amber waves of grain, shining sea

Day 5 A.   It sounds like the author is expressing appreciation for the abundance of America.

They sound like a prayer.

B.   8 syllables, 6 syllables, 8, 6, 8, 6, 8, 6.
grain, plain, thee, sea

LESSON 17

David Livingstone – Foe of Darkness
by Jeannette Eaton

Altogether different was the reception given him a week later by an important chief. **This native was enchanted to see a white man and very curious to know what brought him to a section where only traders had ever come.** David told him of his mission and the chief begged to learn about the white man's God.

Text excerpt, pg. 52 from *David Livingstone - Foe of Darkness,* by Jeannette Eaton. Copyright © 1947 by William Morrow & Company, Inc. By permission of William Morrow & Company, Inc.

DAY 1

A. Read the passage silently. Ask your teacher to help you with difficult words. When you are ready, read the passage out loud to your teacher. In your own words, tell your teacher what is happening in this passage.

B. As your teacher reads the lines in bold print out loud,* write them down. Compare your copy to the passage on this page and make corrections.

NOTE TO THE TEACHER: Spelling lists will be made of unknown words, misspelled words from dictation, and any unknown words from the word study activities. Please do not make weekly lists of more than 5 words. Keep track of words you do not cover and add them to later lists. Keep a list of these words from week to week, noting when they are mastered. Sheets for this purpose are found in the Appendix of this book and in the Student Activity Book.

DAY 2

A. When verbs (action words) tell us about something that has already happened, we say it is in the past tense. The usual way to make a verb show that something has already happened is to add the suffix -ed to the end. Here are some examples: talk, talked; look, looked; jump, jumped. Find the two verbs in our passage that show past tense by adding -ed. Point them out to your teacher.

*This is on the optional Dictation Tape.

56

B. When a verb is made past tense in another way, we say it is irregular. Here are some examples: get, got; sing, sang; run, ran. Find the irregular past tense forms of these verbs in your passage:

is _____   give _____   bring _____   tell _____

C. These sentences are written in the past tense, showing that the action has already happened. Rewrite these sentences in the present tense. Use verbs that show that the action is happening right now.

1. David told him of his mission and the chief begged to learn about the white man's God.

2. The student read the passage about David Livingstone and thought about his mission.

DAY 3

A. David Livingstone's upbringing and education influenced him to decide to become a doctor. He wanted to be a doctor so he could go into unexplored areas and do the work of a missionary. Look up the noun "missionary" in the dictionary. Tell your teacher what a missionary is, and what he tries to do. The word missionary has the word mission as its base. Look up the word mission and write a definition for it that relates to the work of the church.

B. There are three words in our passage that end with the sound /shun/. Find them and write them in a list. There are four letters at the end of each word that spell the sound /shun/. Underline these last four letters in each word on your list. Tell your teacher the two ways to spell this sound.

C. Read the following list of words to your teacher. Notice that each word ends with the /shun/ sound. Though some of these words may be long, the syllables in these words are easy to hear. Try to spell these words orally for your teacher after she reads each one to you. If this is difficult, ask your teacher to read them slowly, emphasizing each syllable. Try to use these words in a writing assignment so you will become more comfortable writing and reading them.

information   vacation   division
civilization   definition

DAY 4

A. Research is the process of looking for information in books like encyclopedias, dictionaries, or resource books. Normally, we research a particular subject.

Do research to try to locate some basic information about David Livingstone. Look for information about his life and work in Africa. Encyclopedias have information on him, as do books about him or his African explorations. If a library is available to you, go there and use the card catalog (either an actual card catalog or computer) to locate resources on David Livingstone. Find two or three of these books, with your teacher's help.

B. There are some basic facts about David Livingstone's life that can be determined by answering the following questions. Answer these questions in writing, but use brief answers that are not complete sentences.

1. Why did Dr. Livingstone go to Africa?
2. What were his most important discoveries?
3. What famous meeting occurred between Dr. Livingstone and another man?
4. How do you think Dr. Livingstone would want to be remembered?

C. Using the answers to these questions, write a paragraph about David Livingstone. The first sentence will be your topic sentence, so make up a sentence that tells what the paragraph is about. Then make up three sentences that tell details about Livingstone's life.

DAY 5

A. Listen as your teacher reads the passage you are to write from dictation.* Do not write as it is read the first time, just listen. Remember, writing from dictation is a skill you acquire with practice, like hitting a baseball. Your first attempts may not be too successful, but as you practice you will become better.

B. After you listen to the passage the second time, write what you have heard. When you have finished, compare your copy to the passage at the beginning of this lesson.

C. Listen as your teacher dictates the spelling words you have been working on this week. Write each word as she reads it to you. After you write each word, use it in a sentence orally. When you are finished, compare your spellings to the correct spellings on your list, and make any needed corrections.

*This is on the optional Dictation Tape.

NOTE TO THE TEACHER: Be sure to add correctly spelled words to a master list that you keep for each student. Record the date the words are correctly spelled.

Teacher Helps:

Day 2 A.   enchanted, begged

B.   was, gave, brought, told

C.   1. David tells him of his mission and the chief begs to learn about the white man's God.

2. The student reads the passage about David Livingstone and thinks about his mission.

Day 3 B.   reception, section, mission

tion, sion

Day 4 B.   1. He came to Africa as a medical missionary in 1840.
2. He discovered Victoria Falls, and was the first man to explore the Zambezi River and Lake Nyasa. He also was the first to cross the continent of Africa.
3. Henry Stanley was sent to find Livingstone, who people thought was dead. When they met he said, "Dr. Livingstone, I presume?"
4. Though he made many famous discoveries, his first love was preaching, teaching and helping the sick.

LESSON 18

One afternoon David sat with him under a great baobab tree. The chief was full of praise for the English doctor's skill in curing a young tribesman of a badly infected wound.

Then suddenly the chief flung out both his hands in passionate entreaty. "I wish you would change my heart. Give me medicine to change it, for it is proud and angry, angry always."

Text excerpt, pg. 52 from *David Livingstone - Foe of Darkness,* by Jeannette Eaton. Copyright © 1947 by William Morrow & Company, Inc. By permission of William Morrow & Company, Inc.

DAY 1

A. Read the passage silently. Ask your teacher to help you with difficult words. When you are ready, read the passage out loud to your teacher. In your own words, tell your teacher what is happening in this passage.

B. As your teacher reads the lines in bold print out loud,* write them down. Compare your copy to the passage on this page and make corrections.

NOTE TO THE TEACHER: Spelling lists will be made of unknown words, misspelled words from dictation, and any unknown words from the word study activities. Please do not make weekly lists of more than 5 words. Keep track of words you do not cover and add them to later lists. Keep a list of these words from week to week, noting when they are mastered. Sheets for this purpose are found in the Appendix of this book and in the Student Activity Book.

DAY 2

A. Some words are spelled in unusual ways, so sayings are made up that help us remember a spelling rule. Here is one of those sayings: "I before e, except after c."

There are a few exceptions to this rule, but most words follow it. Find the word in our passage that follows this rule.

*This is on the optional Dictation Tape.

B. Repeat the saying for your teacher, then tell your teacher the vowel sound in the word "chief." Read this list of words for your teacher, pronouncing the letters ie with a long e sound:

retrieve	thief	grief
field	believe	grieve

C. Use each of the words in a written sentence. Spell all six words orally for your teacher. Ask your teacher to add these words to your spelling list, if needed.

DAY 3

A. In the second part of our passage, the chief asks David for medicine to change his heart. Tell your teacher why you think he asks David for this medicine. Reread the first part of the passage for a clue to the answer.

B. Why does the chief want his heart to be changed? What is he trying to change?

C. How does the chief seem to feel about what he is saying to David? There are two words that give us clues — "passionate entreaty." Look these two words up in the dictionary and tell your teacher how you think the chief feels.

DAY 4

A. Look at the map of Africa in your atlas or the Appendix. Find the compass and point it out to your teacher. This is a common item on most maps.

There are two main types of maps: political (which include divisions for countries) and physical (which show land formations like mountains). You will need an atlas, almanac or other book with a detailed map of Africa as a reference. Write the following locations on your map of the continent of Africa in pencil:

Atlantic Ocean   Indian Ocean   Red Sea   Mediterranean Sea

B. Locate Cape Town on your map. Place a dot there and label it. Locate these other places of interest Dr. Livingstone's explorations:

Victoria Falls   Zambezi River   Lake Nyasa (also know as Lake Malawi)

What present-day countries are these sites located in or near?

C. Livingstone is also known as the first white man to cross Africa. He began in Cape Town and took four years to reach Quelimane, which was a Portuguese settlement on the east coast of Africa. Try to find Quelimane on a map of Africa.

D. Add as many of these main features to your map as you can: The Nile River and the present day names of countries. If the countries on your map are too small, you can write the names on the ocean area with a line pointing to the country.

DAY 5

A. Listen as your teacher reads the passage you are to write from dictation.* Do not write as it is read the first time, just listen. Remember, writing from dictation is a skill you acquire with practice, like hitting a baseball. Your first attempts may not be too successful, but as you practice you will become better.

B. After you listen to the passage the second time, write what you have heard. When you have finished, compare your copy to the passage at the beginning of this lesson.

C. Listen as your teacher dictates the spelling words you have been working on this week. Write each word as she reads it to you. After you write each word, use it in a sentence orally. When you are finished, compare your spellings to the correct spellings on your list, and make any needed corrections.

NOTE TO THE TEACHER: Be sure to add correctly spelled words to a master list that you keep for each student. Record the date the words are correctly spelled.

*This is on the optional Dictation Tape.

Teacher Helps:

Day 2 A. *Learning Grammar Through Writing,* 11k.
chief

    B. long e

Day 3 A. The chief saw David use medicine to heal a tribesman.

    B. His heart is proud and angry, and these are feelings he wants to be gone from his heart.

Day 4 A., B., C.

LESSON 19

Looking into the glowing dark eyes, David said gently, "If you will let the loving spirit of Christ enter your heart, it will be changed."

"Nay!" cried the chief and beat his breast with both hands. "I wish to have it changed by medicine and to have it changed at once, for it is always very proud and very uneasy and continually angry with someone."

Text excerpt, pg. 52 from *David Livingstone - Foe of Darkness,* by Jeannette Eaton. Copyright © 1947 by William Morrow & Company, Inc. By permission of William Morrow & Company, Inc.

DAY 1

A. Read the passage silently. Ask your teacher to help you with difficult words. When you are ready, read the passage out loud to your teacher. In your own words, tell your teacher what is happening in this passage.

B. As your teacher reads the lines in bold print out loud,* write them down. Compare your copy to the passage on this page and make corrections.

NOTE TO THE TEACHER: Spelling lists will be made of unknown words, misspelled words from dictation, and any unknown words from the word study activities. Please do not make weekly lists of more than 5 words. Keep track of words you do not cover and add them to later lists. Keep a list of these words from week to week, noting when they are mastered. Sheets for this purpose are found in the Appendix of this book and in the Student Activity Book.

DAY 2

A. Many parts of our passage are words that were spoken by someone. To show that these words were spoken, we surround those words with marks called quotation marks. Find the exact words that were spoken by David Livingstone and underline them with a red pencil or pen.

B. Using a blue pencil or pen, underline the exact words spoken by the chief. His words are divided into two sentences, so be sure to mark only the words he said. Look at both underlined passages. Find the punctuation marks at the end of each sentence. Are they inside the quotation marks, or outside? Punctuation marks are usually included inside the closing quotation marks.

*This is on the optional Dictation Tape.

C. Listen to a conversation between two members of your family, and try to write down three or four sentences from their discussion. (The best way to get all the words both people speak is to tape record the conversation, with their permission of course.) As you write the conversation down, you will need to add descriptions such as Mom said, or Bill asked. If you just write down what they said, it will be difficult to understand who is speaking. Remember to put quotation marks in where they are needed.

DAY 3

A. In the last part of our passage the word easy has been used, with a prefix added to it. Find this word and tell your teacher what the prefix is and what you think it means.

B. Prefixes are added to the front of base words, and they change the meanings of the words. Look at this picture of a house that demonstrates adding prefixes and suffixes.

Rewrite these words adding the prefix un- to each one.

          happy   tie   paid   like

Tell your teacher how you think the prefix un- changes the meanings of these words.

C. Rewrite these sentences using a word with the prefix un- attached to it:

    The road is not very even.
    I am not certain about the weather.
    Mom said the chair was not comfortable.

Make up three more sentences using a word that includes the prefix un-. Look in the dictionary under un- if you are having trouble thinking of words.

DAY 4

A. Reread the passages for Lesson 18 and for this lesson. Read them for your teacher. Although the chief wants medicine to cure his angry heart, what does David tell the chief he must do to cure his heart? Discuss with your teacher the message that David Livingstone told the chief.

B. What response does the chief give David? Does the chief accept David's advice? Why not?

C. Discuss with your teacher the emotions behind the words in this week's Lesson. Which word tells you how David spoke to the chief? Say the exact words David spoke, with the tone of voice you think he used.

Which words and phrases in the Lesson tell you how the chief spoke his response? Say the words of the chief, with the tone of voice you think he used. You may act out the chief's words if you would like.

DAY 5

A. Listen as your teacher reads the passage you are to write from dictation.* Do not write as it is read the first time, just listen. Remember, writing from dictation is a skill you acquire with practice, like hitting a baseball. Your first attempts may not be too successful, but as you practice you will become better.

B. After you listen to the passage the second time, write what you have heard. When you have finished, compare your copy to the passage at the beginning of this lesson.

C. Listen as your teacher dictates the spelling words you have been working on this week. Write each word as she reads it to you. After you write each word, use it in a sentence orally. When you are finished, compare your spellings to the correct spellings on your list, and make any needed corrections.

NOTE TO THE TEACHER: Be sure to add correctly spelled words to a master list that you keep for each student. Record the date the words are correctly spelled.

Teacher Helps:

Day 2 A.   *Learning Grammar Through Writing,* 10t.

"If you will let the loving spirit of Christ enter your heart, it will be changed."

   B.   There are two periods and an exclamation point.

Learning Grammar Through Writing, 10v.

Day 3 A.   un – It means not.

   B.   unhappy, untie, unpaid, unlike

   C.   The road is uneven
I am uncertain about the weather.
Mom said the chair was uncomfortable.

Day 4 A.   David told the chief that he must "let the loving spirit of Christ" enter his heart.

   B.   The chief's response is "Nay!" He does not accept David's advice. He prefers to have medicine change his heart so that his heart will be changed immediately.

   C.   David spoke his words "gently."

The chief "cried" as he spoke. He beat his breast with both hands.

LESSON 20

David smiled pityingly at this very human wish for a quick dose of holiness. "Alas, medicine heals only the body. Love, a thing of the spirit, must push anger from your heart."

Text excerpt, pg. 52 from *David Livingstone - Foe of Darkness,* by Jeannette Eaton. Copyright © 1947 by William Morrow & Company, Inc. By permission of William Morrow & Company, Inc.

DAY 1

A. Read the passage silently. Ask your teacher to help you with difficult words. When you are ready, read the passage out loud to your teacher. In your own words, tell your teacher what is happening in this passage.

B. As your teacher reads the lines in bold print out loud,* write them down. Compare your copy to the passage on this page and make corrections.

NOTE TO THE TEACHER: Spelling lists will be made of unknown words, misspelled words from dictation, and any unknown words from the word study activities. Please do not make weekly lists of more than 5 words. Keep track of words you do not cover and add them to later lists. Keep a list of these words from week to week, noting when they are mastered. Sheets for this purpose are found in the Appendix of this book and in the Student Activity Book.

DAY 2

A. Suffixes are endings we add to words to change their meanings. We start with a base word, and then add a suffix. Here is a picture:

In this lesson, find the word with the base word "holy" with a suffix added to it. Be careful, because the spelling of the word "holy" was changed to add the suffix. Circle the word.

B. Can you make up a rule about adding the suffix -ness to a word that ends with a consonant and a "y"? Spell these base words after adding the suffix -ness for your teacher orally:

        happy   good   kind   lazy

*This is on the optional Dictation Tape.

C. What do you think the suffix -ness means? Listen to your teacher read this sentence and tell her what you think the suffix -ness means:

We all noticed her kindness.

Write a sentence with each of the words you made in activity B today.

BONUS QUESTION: Look at the word "pityingly" in our passage and tell your teacher why the "y" was left on the end of pity when we added suffixes to it.

DAY 3

A. Review the definitions we have previously learned about adverbs: that they tell us how, when, where or how much something was done. Adverbs often end with the letters -ly. The word "very" is usually an adverb because it tells us how much there is of something. Underline the adverbs in this passage with a red pencil.

B. Jeanette Eaton, the author of *David Livingstone – Foe of Darkness*, uses a dramatic style in her writing. Her use of adverbs and adjectives helps us understand her meaning. Look back over the four passages from her in Lessons 17–20 of this (Purple) book and choose three sentences that you think are very descriptive and well written. Copy them on a piece of paper, leaving a blank line between them.

C. Using colored pencils, underline the adjectives in red. Try to think of a synonym (word close to the same meaning) for each adjective. If you need help, you can use a dictionary or thesaurus.

Next, underline the adverbs in blue. Try to find a synonym for each adverb if you can. Read the sentence or phrase using the synonyms. Remember these adjectives, adverbs and synonyms when you write. Try to use at least one new word each week either in your writing or speaking.

DAY 4

A. David Livingstone said of himself, "I am a missionary, heart and soul." He is well known for all of his explorations and discoveries in Africa, but he also said that this was not what was most important to him. In this passage, we see a missionary's heart towards those he talks with. Describe David's attitude toward the chief.

B. If you know any missionaries personally, ask them to tell you about their goals, travels, and how their lives have been different from other families. Ask them what they have done that they feel has helped people. If you do not know any missionaries personally, perhaps you have family members or friends who can tell you about missionaries they have known.

C. There have been many famous missionaries who have traveled to different parts of the world to tell people about the Gospel. If you would like, you can study a missionary in greater detail. Using library books or books your family owns, look for stories about missionaries. Choose one missionary, read about him or her, and then tell your family about his or her life. Here are some suggestions, if you can't think of one:

> Eric Liddell (missionary to China)
> Amy Carmichael (missionary to India)
> Billy Graham (evangelist to the world)
> Apostle Paul (missionary to Greece, Rome)

DAY 5

A. Listen as your teacher reads the passage you are to write from dictation.* Do not write as it is read the first time, just listen. Remember, writing from dictation is a skill you acquire with practice, like hitting a baseball. Your first attempts may not be too successful, but as you practice you will become better.

B. After you listen to the passage the second time, write what you have heard. When you have finished, compare your copy to the passage at the beginning of this lesson.

C. Listen as your teacher dictates the spelling words you have been working on this week. Write each word as she reads it to you. After you write each word, use it in a sentence orally. When you are finished, compare your spellings to the correct spellings on your list, and make any needed corrections.

NOTE TO THE TEACHER: Be sure to add correctly spelled words to a master list that you keep for each student. Record the date the words are correctly spelled.

Teacher Helps:

Day 2 A.   holiness

B.   When a base word ends in a consonant and a "y," and you add a suffix that begins with any letter but "i," you change the "y" to and "i" before adding the suffix. (*Learning Grammar Through Writing,* 11h.)

happiness, goodness, kindness, laziness

C.   The suffix -ness means having the quality of the base word. For example, "goodness" means having the quality of being "good."

BONUS   Because the suffix -ing begins with the letter "i." (*Learning Grammar Through Writing,* 11h.)

Day 3 A.   pityingly, very

B. & C.   Answers will vary depending upon the sentences chosen.

Day 4 A.   David was very compassionate and understanding of the chief's feelings.

LESSON 21

DAY 1

Several weeks ago in Lesson 8 you spent a week preparing a read aloud presentation. Talk to your teacher about that experience. What did you enjoy about it? What did you not like about it?

This week you will work with one or more other people to prepare a choral reading presentation. This type of presentation can feel more comfortable because you have others standing with you before the audience. Preparation is still very important.

The first step is to choose the others who will read with you. You may include your teacher, too. You may use as many people as you wish, but no more than four is suggested for one week of preparation.

Secondly, determine your audience and the type of material they will enjoy hearing. Since you are working with other readers, you may choose a longer piece than you used last time.

DAY 2

Meet with all the readers, and read over your chosen material to learn the meaning of it. Talk to your teacher about words you do not understand. Try to find out what the author wanted to communicate.

Read the material again looking for the emotion (feelings) behind the words. Did the author want us to laugh, cry, learn, etc. when we read this work? Talk to your teacher about how you might use your voice to express these feelings. Ask these questions:

1. What will we emphasize as we speak?
2. Where will we pause as we speak?
3. Will we use our voices in any other manner to communicate the meaning?

If you will be presenting a story, your group may need to use different kinds of voices for each character. Ask these questions:

1. What do we need to emphasize?
2. Where do we need to pause?
3. How do we need to use our voice to communicate the meaning?

In choral readings you must decide which lines will be read by whom and which lines will be read by everyone. Many times the lines that need emphasis are read by everyone.

Look at the following Psalm and read it aloud as directed. That will help you get the feel of choral reading. The example is given for four readers. If you have more or fewer you may adapt it.

If you have 2 readers -
    Reader #1 - reads 1 & 3
    Reader #2 - reads 2 & 4

If you have 3 readers -
    Reader # 1 - reads 1 & #4's He guides me...
    Reader # 2 - reads 2 & #4's Thy rod...
    Reader # 3 - reads 3 & #4's Surely, goodness...

PSALM 24:2

ALL:	The Lord is my shepherd, I shall not want.
Person 1:	He makes me lie down in green pastures;
Person 2:	He leads me beside quiet waters.
Person 3:	He restores my soul;
Person 4:	He guides me in the paths of righteousness
ALL:	For His name's sake.
Person 1:	Even though I walk through the valley of the shadow of death,
Person 2:	I fear no evil;
Person 3:	For Thou art with me;
Person 4:	Thy rod and Thy staff, they comfort me.
Person 1:	Thou dost prepare a table before me in the presence of my enemies;
Person 2:	Thou has anointed my head with oil;
Person 3:	My cup overflows.
Person 4:	Surely *(pause)* goodness and loving kindness will follow me all the days of my life,
ALL:	And I will dwell in the house of the Lord forever.

Assign parts for the material you have chosen to present. You may want to copy the material for each reader and let each reader mark his or her part.

DAYS 3 & 4

Practice reading your material aloud at least three times each day. You are not required to memorize the entire passage, however, you should know it well enough to be able to look up from your book several times during the presentation.

Stand in front of a mirror as you practice. Use the following list to help you evaluate yourself. After you have practiced several times, ask your teacher or another student to evaluate you, using the list.

____ 1. Do we read slowly?
____ 2. Do we read clearly?
____ 3. Do we read loud enough?
____ 4. Are we using our voices well to communicate the meaning and feeling?
____ 5. Are we standing up straight, but naturally?
____ 6. Do we look at our audience enough?

Decide how all the readers will stand as they present their reading. You may form a pattern, depending on the height of the readers.

Example:
    Be sure the audience can see everyone and everyone can see the audience. Taller readers should be in the back while shorter readers should be in front.

O O — Taller Readers
O   O

Audience

The readers may hold scripts in their hands, or a large print of the reading can be held up in the back of the room.

DAY 5

Your presentation day has arrived, and even though you may feel nervous, you are ready for your audience because you planned for it. If you feel very nervous, ask your teacher to sit in the back of the room and give you support by smiling at you.

LESSON 22

DAY 1

Listen as your teacher reads *The History of Strawberry Girl* found in the Appendix.*
Talk with your teacher about the main points of the history.
  1. Who was Lois Lenski?
  2. What is the story of *Strawberry Girl*?
  3. How did the growing of strawberries become a success in Florida?

DAY 2

A. Reread the seventh paragraph of *The History of Strawberry Girl*. Read the following outline of this paragraph. Find the sentence from which each item on the outline was taken.

  I. Achieving successful strawberry growing.
   A. Rich soil needed
   B. Mild Central Florida weather
   C. The help of Mr. Henry Plant

  II. Strawberry growing started in 1881 by settlers from Mississippi.
   A. Climate allowed plants to be set out in fall
   B. Harvest begun as early as January

  III. A new industry is born.

B. Using the above outline, rewrite the paragraph, using your own words. When you are finished, compare your paragraph to the original paragraph. See if you can find differences. Does your paragraph tell the story just as well?

DAY 3

A. Using an atlas or encyclopedia, look at a map of Florida. Locate the cities mentioned in *The History of Strawberry Girl*:

  Lakeland   Tampa

These cities are located in Central Florida. Show your teacher where you think these three locations and their cities would be on the map of Florida found in the Appendix:

*This is on the optional Dictation Tape.

<u>Northern Florida</u>	Pensacola, Tallahassee, Jacksonville
<u>Central Florida</u>	Orlando, Melbourne
<u>Southern Florida</u>	Ft. Lauderdale, Miami

Many states or countries are divided into northern, central and southern areas. This is common map terminology.

B. Look up a map of your state and find the northern, central and southern sections. Identify one city in each region. (If you live in Florida, you may want to get a map of your city and find a street in the northern, central and southern parts of your city.)

C. Look at a map of the continental United States (not including Alaska and Hawaii.) The United States is usually thought of more in terms of eastern, central and western states. Find states that would be considered a part of each classification: eastern, central and western.

For a more complex identification, two directions can be combined. Looking at the compass on the map, find these directions:

   northeast
   northwest
   southeast
   southwest

Find a state that you think would fall into each one of those directional categories: northeast, northwest, southeast and southwest.

DAY 4

A. Reread the 8th paragraph of *The History of Strawberry Girl*, found in the Appendix. Talk to your teacher about the two main points of the paragraph. On a sheet of paper, copy the following outline, or use the outline found in the Student Activity Book.

   I.

      A.

      B.

   II.

      A.

      B.

Using phrases (not complete sentences), write the first main point of the paragraph next to Roman numeral One (I.). Write the second main point next to Roman numeral Two (II.).

Reread the paragraph, looking for at least two details about each main point. Write the details next to the letters A. and B. in your outline.

B. Give your outline to your teacher. Ask your teacher to tell you what the paragraph is about, using only your outline. Was your teacher able to discover the main points of the paragraph from your outline? Discuss this with your teacher, and change some points of your outline if you and your teacher feel you should.

DAY 5

A. Using the outline you wrote yesterday, rewrite the paragraph. Try to include as much detail as you can remember.

B. When you are finished, compare your paragraph to the original. Did you include all of the same main points? What about details—did you include as many as the original paragraph? You may want to revise your outline to include any main items you did not include.

C. Try this procedure with another paragraph from any book you would like. Try to find a different type of writing, if possible. Directions, telling how to do something, are very good to outline because they make clear-cut points. Outline first, and then try to rewrite the paragraph. Compare your paragraph to the original and make needed changes.

Teacher Helps:

Day 3 A.

Day 4 A.   I. Transporting the strawberries
         A. Central Florida railroad connected east & west coasts of Florida
         B. Strawberries, packed in ice, were shipped up North

       II. Harvesting the strawberries
         A. "Strawberry school" closed during harvest time
         B. The whole family worked in times of frost

LESSON 23

Strawberry Girl
by Lois Lenski

Mr. Boyer had sent word to all the neighbors that he was grinding cane. People began to drop in—the Tatums, the Cooks and others. The men went to the field where they cut the long cane stalks and hauled them in. They took turns feeding the stalks into the rollers. Cane pulp, called "pummy" fell to the ground at one side.

The pale green milky-looking cane juice poured out slowly into a barrel on the other side. Flies began to come, attracted by its sweetness. Like the flies, children and grown-ups came too, <u>all</u> eager to taste.

Selection reprinted from *Strawberry Girl* ©1945
by permission of the Lois Lenski Covey Foundation, Inc.

DAY 1

A. Read the passage silently. Ask your teacher to help you with difficult words. When you are ready, read the passage out loud to your teacher. In your own words, tell your teacher what is happening in this passage.

B. As your teacher reads the lines in bold print out loud,* write them down. Compare your copy to the passage on this page and make corrections.

NOTE TO THE TEACHER: Spelling lists will be made of unknown words, misspelled words from dictation, and any unknown words from the word study activities. Please do not make weekly lists of more than 5 words. Keep track of words you do not cover and add them to later lists. Keep a list of these words from week to week, noting when they are mastered. Sheets for this purpose are found in the Appendix of this book and in the Student Activity Book.

DAY 2

A. Listen as your teacher rereads the last two sentences of the passage. The last sentence is a comparison of two things that shows how they are alike. This is called a simile (sim-e-lee). Similes use the words "like" or "as" to show how two things are alike. Look at the sentences again and tell your teacher what two things are alike.

*This is on the optional Dictation Tape.

B. Similes often paint word pictures to help us understand what a writer is trying to say. Read these similes to your teacher.

> The children were as busy as bees.
> Your hands are as cold as ice.
> He drives like a race car driver.
> The room feels like an oven.

Tell your teacher the quality that both people or things share in each simile above.

C. Make up two similes using like and two similes using as. Remember that comparing things to animals, or things in nature is often a good way to start. Here are two similes with blanks in them. If you use these to help you, still make two more of each.

> a ____ is as gentle as a lamb.
> _____ sleeps like a baby.

DAY 3

A. There are several words in our passage that have the broad sound of "a" that says /awe/. This sound is spelled several different ways. Reread your passage and try to find the words that have the sound /awe/ spelled with "a" and another letter.

B. Write these three headings on the top of a piece of paper or use your Student Activity Book:

<u>al</u>   <u>aw</u>   <u>au</u>

The following words contain letters that are like the three headings you made (above.) Write each of these words under the heading with the same spelling of /awe/ sound as is found in the word.

fall	saw	cause
auto	talk	lawn
crawl	taunt	small

The vowel sound in these words sounds very similar, yet is spelled three different ways. Practice spelling these words out loud to your teacher. Try to memorize at least three words that use each spelling. For the next few days, ask your teacher to call out these words individually and tell her either al, aw, or au. As you read other words using these spellings, add them to your list with the three categories.

DAY 4

A. Our passage gives us an idea of the steps involved in grinding sugar cane. What is sugar cane? What do we get from sugar cane? Look "sugar cane" up in an encyclopedia or dictionary.

Sugar cane is a common crop in Florida, Hawaii and other places with warm climates. Talk with your teacher about why you think sugar cane was important to the people of Central Florida.

B. Mr. Boyer has a sugar cane mill. Make a list, using numbers, like this:

    1.
    2.
    3.

and tell the steps it takes to get "pummy" and cane juice.

C. Write a paragraph telling how to make sugar cane juice. Sometimes the words first, next and then (or first, second and thirdly) help you write when you are telling about a step-by-step process. Look at your list after you have written your paragraph to make sure you included all the steps.

DAY 5

A. Listen as your teacher reads the passage you are to write from dictation.* Do not write as it is read the first time, just listen. Remember, writing from dictation is a skill you acquire with practice it, like hitting a baseball. Your first attempts may not be too successful, but as you practice you will become better.

B. After you listen to the passage the second time, write what you have heard. When you have finished, compare your copy to the passage at the beginning of this lesson.

C. Listen as your teacher dictates the spelling words you have been working on this week. Write each word as she reads it to you. After you write each word, use it in a sentence orally. When you are finished, compare your spellings to the correct spellings on your list, and make any needed corrections.

NOTE TO THE TEACHER: Be sure to add correctly spelled words to a master list that you keep for each student. Record the date the words are correctly spelled.

Teacher Helps:

Day 2 A. The flies, and the children and grown-ups, all drawn by the sweetness.

B. Children and bees are busy.
Hands and ice are cold.
"He" and the race car driver drive alike (fast).
The room and the oven feel the same (warm).

Day 3 A. all, stalks, hauled

B.

al	aw	au
fall	saw	cause
talk	lawn	auto
small	crawl	taunt

Day 4 B.
1. cut stalks from the field
2. haul stalks to mill
3. feed stalks into rollers

C. Making sugar cane takes three steps. First you must cut stalks from the field. Next you haul the stalks to the mill. Then you feed the stalks into the rollers.

LESSON 24

She found Dovey and took the three little girls to a shady spot under the big umbrella tree. She made play dollies out of towels for them. She brought sugar cane, peeled it down and gave them pieces to suck and chew. She promised them candy at the candy-pulling in the evening.

With a piece of sugar cane in her mouth, she ran back to the mill. Semina was still making her obedient rounds. The mule walked with her eyes closed as if she could go on forever.

Selection reprinted from *Strawberry Girl* ©1945
by permission of the Lois Lenski Covey Foundation, Inc.

DAY 1

A. Read the passage silently. Ask your teacher to help you with difficult words. When you are ready, read the passage out loud to your teacher. In your own words, tell your teacher what is happening in this passage.

B. As your teacher reads the lines in bold print out loud,* write them down. Compare your copy to the passage on this page and make corrections.

NOTE TO THE TEACHER: Spelling lists will be made of unknown words, misspelled words from dictation, and any unknown words from the word study activities. Please do not make weekly lists of more than 5 words. Keep track of words you do not cover and add them to later lists. Keep a list of these words from week to week, noting when they are mastered. Sheets for this purpose are found in the Appendix of this book and in the Student Activity Book.

DAY 2

A. When something has already happened, we say the verb, or doing word is in the past tense. Here are some examples:

The dog runs to the house.
(Happening now. Present tense.)

The dog ran to the house.
(Already happened. Past tense.)

*This is on the optional Dictation Tape.

In our passage, many of the verbs are written in past tense. Find the doing words (verbs), and show them to your teacher. Make a vertical list of the words you find.

B. Read each word on your list. These words are past tense, meaning they show that these actions have already happened. Think about each word. Next to each word on your list, write the word that would show that the action is happening right now. (present tense) Here are some examples:

bought	(past tense)	buys	(present tense)
said	(past tense)	says	(present tense)
drove	(past tense)	drives	(present tense)
looked	(past tense)	looks	(present tense)

C. Rewrite the first paragraph of our passage, replacing the past tense verbs from your list with the present tense verbs.

Read it to your teacher. Make any needed corrections. Make sure each sentence sounds correct to you.

DAY 3

A. Do you know what a hyphen is? A hyphen is used to connect words or to divide them. There are many reasons to use a hyphen. Three of those reasons are:

1 - To connect some compound words.
2 - To connect some number words and fractions.
3 - To connect some describing words (adjectives).

Look at the following words and tell your teacher which of the above reasons explains why the hyphen is used in each word:

teen-ager	thirty-seven
one-half	well-to-do

B. Look in our passage for this week. Find the hyphenated word and tell your teacher why the hyphen is used.

C. Hyphens are also used to divide a word when it will not fit on one line and it must be continued on the next line. When words are divided in this way, the hyphen must be used between syllables.

Look at the passage on the top of page 79, and find three words that use a hyphen. Tell your teacher why each one has a hyphen.

D. Dividing words into syllables when they won't fit on one line is one of the most common uses of the hyphen. Look at any book or newspaper. Find three examples of words being divided from the end of one line to the beginning of the next line with a hyphen. Show these to your teacher.

Look at the following words. Write them on a separate sheet, or in your Student Activity Book, showing where each word would be divided if it would not fit on one line.

obedient	little
umbrella	promised
making	forever
under	towel
sugar	

Sometime soon, try to use a hyphen to divide a word into syllables in your writing. You can check the proper place to divide the syllables of a word by looking it up in the dictionary.

DAY 4

A. The main character of the story *Strawberry Girl* is a young girl named Birdie Boyer. Lois Lenski, the author of *Strawberry Girl* also wrote a book of poems called *Florida, My Florida*. In this book, a poem about Birdie and her family is included. It is entitled *Cracker Girl*. Listen as your teacher reads this poem* (found in the Appendix.) As you listen, notice how the language that is used is different from the way you speak.

B. Read the poem silently after your teacher has read it. Ask your teacher about any words or expressions that are unknown to you. Then read the poem aloud to your teacher. Practice a few times. How does it feel to read language that is different? This type of language is called informal, slang, or dialect. That means it is language that is written in the same way a people from a certain part of the country, a certain time period, or a certain culture might speak. It is different from standard English we use in most speaking and writing. It often shows us a unique quality of a group of people.

*This is on the optional Dictation Tape.

Talk with your teacher about the area where you live. Are there any examples of unique dialects around you? See if you can find stories or poems written in a dialect or informal language common to your area. Your librarian may be able to help you find such poems or stories.

C. Practice reading *Cracker Girl*, and present it to your family. Try to read it with expression in your voice, as if you were speaking in your own dialect.

DAY 5

A. Listen as your teacher reads the passage you are to write from dictation.* Do not write as it is read the first time, just listen. Remember, writing from dictation is a skill you acquire with practice, like hitting a baseball. Your first attempts may not be too successful, but as you practice you will become better.

B. After you listen to the passage the second time, write what you have heard. When you have finished, compare your copy to the passage at the beginning of this lesson.

C. Listen as your teacher dictates the spelling words you have been working on this week. Write each word as she reads it to you. After you write each word, use it in a sentence orally. When you are finished, compare your spellings to the correct spellings on your list, and make any needed corrections.

NOTE TO THE TEACHER: Be sure to add correctly spelled words to a mastery list that you keep for each student. Record the date the words are correctly spelled.

Teacher Helps:

Day 2 A.   found, took, made, brought, peeled, gave, promised, ran, was, walked

     B.

found – finds	took – takes
made – makes	brought – brings
peeled – peels	gave – gives
promised – promises	ran – runs
was – is	walked – walks

     C.   She finds Dovey and takes the three little girls to a shady spot under the big umbrella tree. She makes play dollies out of towels for them. She brings sugar cane, peels it down and gives them pieces to suck and chew. She promises them candy at the candy-pulling in the evening.

Day 3 A.   teenager / compound word
thirty-seven / number word
one-half / fraction word
well-to-do / adjective

     B.   candy-pulling / It is a compound word.

     C.   milky-looking / adjective
grown-ups / compound word
bar-rel / won't fit on one line

     D.

o-be-di-ent	lit-tle
um-brel-la	prom-ised
mak-ing	for-ev-er
un-der	tow-el
sug-ar	

Day 4 A.   young uns, stretch o ground, we was fixing, to make us a good livin, neighbors made a ruckus, etc.

LESSON 25

At dusk-dark the real fun began.

Sam Slater and Gus and Joe appeared. No frolic was complete without them. Sam brought his fiddle into the house and struck up a lively tune, while Shoestring stood at his side and picked on the violin strings with knitting needles, for an accompaniment. **The men and women formed into lines and Sam Slater called the dance steps in a loud voice. Soon the rooms and porches were a flurry of movement, music and laughter.** Joe Slater danced fancy steps, and made the people laugh. "He shore can cut the fool!" they said.

Selection reprinted from *Strawberry Girl* ©1945
by permission of the Lois Lenski Covey Foundation, Inc.

DAY 1

A. Read the passage silently. Ask your teacher to help you with difficult words. When you are ready, read the passage out loud to your teacher. In your own words, tell your teacher what is happening in this passage.

B. As your teacher reads the lines in bold print out loud,* write them down. Compare your copy to the passage on this page and make corrections.

NOTE TO THE TEACHER: Spelling lists will be made of unknown words, misspelled words from dictation, and any unknown words from the word study activities. Please do not make weekly lists of more than 5 words. Keep track of words you do not cover and add them to later lists. Keep a list of these words from week to week, noting when they are mastered. Sheets for this purpose are found in the Appendix of this book and in the Student Activity Book.

DAY 2

A. People who lived in the pioneer days of any land realized that they had to depend on each other for help in times of need and for fun and fellowship. The Slater family causes considerable trouble for the families in the area, particularly the Boyers. This festive event (called a frolic) is being held at the Boyer home, and the Slater boys—Sam, Gus and Joe are there. Read the passage again.   How did the Slaters participate in the frolic?

*This is on the optional Dictation Tape.

B. The dancing that they are doing is probably similar to what we know of as square dancing. Look this up in an encyclopedia and tell your teacher some of the main elements of square dancing—such as how it is done, what kind of music is used, etc.

C. If you have an opportunity, observe or participate in a square dance with your parents' permission and/or by accompanying them. If possible, view a video that shows basic square dancing.

How do you think this type of event was helpful to pioneer people?

DAY 3

A. Listen as your teacher reads the poem entitled *Beholden* by Lois Lenski (found in the Appendix.) Read the poem silently after your teacher has read it.* Looking at the poem, make a list of all the words that seem unusual in their spelling or pronunciation.

B. Talk with your teacher and come up with definitions for each of these dialectal words. Rewrite the poem putting your own words in place of the words on your list. Do you think the poem sounds better with your words, or with the original words?

C. Count the number of syllables in each line and write down the numbers. What is the pattern is for each group of four lines? Think of a familiar topic and try to write four lines about it, following the same syllable pattern, or find another poem that follows the same pattern.

DAY 4

A. Reread the poem *Cracker Girl* by Lois Lenski (found under Lesson 24 in the Appendix.) Look at the last four lines of this poem. The neighbors referred to by Birdie in this poem are the Slaters. What does Birdie say about her mother? Who do you suppose the neighbors are who are told about in the poem entitled *Beholden*?

B. Jesus said "Do unto others as you would have them do unto you." (Luke 6:31) People today call this "the Golden Rule." How do you think Mrs. Boyer has been demonstrating the Golden Rule in her relationship with the Slaters?

What do you think has been the effect of her kindness?

Discuss the Golden Rule with your teacher. Write the Golden Rule on a sheet of paper, or in your Student Activity Book.

C. Can you think of a situation in your life to which you can apply the Golden Rule? Do you think it is always easy to do this? Talk with your teacher about ways you can apply the Golden Rule to a specific situation. You may want to write about that situation, then write about the situation later and tell the results of applying the Golden Rule.

DAY 5

A. Listen as your teacher reads the passage you are to write from dictation.* Do not write as it is read the first time, just listen. Remember, writing from dictation is a skill you acquire with practice, like hitting a baseball. Your first attempts may not be too successful, but as you practice you will become better.

B. After you listen to the passage the second time, write what you have heard. When you have finished, compare your copy to the passage at the beginning of this lesson.

C. Listen as your teacher dictates the spelling words you have been working on this week. Write each word as she reads it to you. After you write each word, use it in a sentence orally. When you are finished, compare your spellings to the correct spellings on your list, and make any needed corrections.

NOTE TO THE TEACHER: Be sure to add correctly spelled words to a master list that you keep for each student. Record the date the words are correctly spelled.

*This is on the optional Dictation Tape.

Teacher Helps:

Day 2 A. The Slaters were a main part of the event, playing music, calling the dance steps and leading the dance.

C. The pioneer life was a hard life full of work, and the people seldom got a chance to get together for relaxation and recreation. These opportunities became important times for pioneer families.

Day 3 A. hit, beholden, porely, young uns, full o meanness, bygones

C. 7, 6, 7, 6

Day 4 A. That her mother showed them a better way

The Slaters and the Boyers.

B. Mrs. Boyer has been doing kind things for the Slaters.

Mrs. Slater has deeply appreciated Mrs. Boyer's kindness.

LESSON 26

Meanwhile Mr. Boyer had set fire to a pine stump near by. **When darkness came down, he had a great bonfire burning to light up the yard. The boys ran to pile on more lightwood knots whenever it burned low. It hissed and crackled and popped, bathing the dancing figures in a pattern of light and shadow.**

Mr. Boyer made the candy himself. He boiled the syrup down to just the right temperature, then poured the thickening mixture out on many plates to cool.

Birdie took plates to the little Slater girls and Dovey and showed them how to pull.

Selection reprinted from *Strawberry Girl* ©1945
by permission of the Lois Lenski Covey Foundation, Inc.

DAY 1

A. Read the passage silently. Ask your teacher to help you with difficult words. When you are ready, read the passage out loud to your teacher. In your own words, tell your teacher what is happening in this passage.

B. As your teacher reads the lines in bold print out loud,* write them down. Compare your copy to the passage on this page and make corrections.

NOTE TO THE TEACHER: Spelling lists will be made of unknown words, misspelled words from dictation, and any unknown words from the word study activities. Please do not make weekly lists of more than 5 words. Keep track of words you do not cover and add them to later lists. Keep a list of these words from week to week, noting when they are mastered. Sheets for this purpose are found in the Appendix of this book and in the Student Activity Book.

DAY 2

A. Compound words are made up of two separate words put together to form a new word such as "baseball." There are five compound words in our passage. Point them out to your teacher.

*This is on the optional Dictation Tape.

B. Two of our compound words have meanings that are very interesting. Look up the words bonfire and lightwood in the dictionary. After reading the definitions, tell your teacher what these words mean.

C. Bonfires can be fun, and the boys seem very excited as they run to add wood to the fire. There are three adjectives (describing words) in our passage that tell about the sounds the fire is making. Find these three words and point them out to your teacher. These are very colorful adjectives. Use these adjectives and any others you can think of to describe a bonfire. Think about any bonfires you have seen, and write several sentences describing what a bonfire looks like and sounds like to you.

DAY 3

In times past, agricultural communities often got together for events relating to harvest time. This passage describes a farming community getting together to participate in, and celebrate harvesting the sugar cane crop. As part of the fun, candy was made with the boiled cane juice. Everyone took a plate of the cooling mixture, which had to be "pulled" to get it ready to eat. Ask if you can make one of these types of candy, with your teacher's assistance and supervision. One recipe that would be very similar to the candy-pulling in our passage would be saltwater taffy. Many cookbooks have recipes for taffy. One recipe is found in the Appendix.

DAY 4

A. Yesterday you used a recipe to make candy. Recipes are written so that you understand what to do step-by-step. Reread the recipe you used to make the candy.

B. Without copying the recipe, use your own words to write several sentences that tell someone how to make the candy you made yesterday. Be as specific as you need to, so that someone else would know exactly what to do.

C. Give your directions and the recipe to your teacher, and ask if you have included all the necessary steps. The best test of your directions would be for someone to use them as directions and try to make the same candy you made. The final test of your directions will be how the candy tastes.

DAY 5

A. Listen as your teacher reads the passage you are to write from dictation.* Do not write as it is read the first time, just listen. Remember, writing from dictation is a skill you acquire with practice, like hitting a baseball. Your first attempts may not be too successful, but as you practice you will become better.

B. After you listen to the passage the second time, write what you have heard. When you have finished, compare your copy to the passage at the beginning of this lesson.

C. Listen as your teacher dictates the spelling words you have been working on this week. Write each word as she reads it to you. After you write each word, use it in a sentence orally. When you are finished, compare your spellings to the correct spellings on your list, and make any needed corrections.

NOTE TO THE TEACHER: Be sure to add correctly spelled words to a mastery list that you keep for each student. Record the date the words are correctly spelled.

Teacher Helps:

Day 2 A.   meanwhile, bonfire, lightwood, whenever, himself

   C.   hissed, crackled, popped

*This is on the optional Dictation Tape.

LESSON 27

Amos Fortune, Free Man
by Elizabeth Yates

Amos and Violet slept under the stars while peepers chimed in a marsh nearby and late birds called to each other. **They were free. They were starting life anew. They were being helped to get going and the people in the land to which they had come were showing gladness at their arrival.**

"God give me strength for many years to do my work well," Amos prayed in the quiet of his heart.

From *Amos Fortune, Free Man* by Elizabeth Yates, cover by Lonnie Knabel. ©1950 by Elizabeth Yates McGreal, renewed ©1978 by Elizabeth Yates McGreal. Used by permission of Dutton Children's Books, a division of Penguin Books USA, Inc.

DAY 1

A. Read the passage silently. Ask your teacher to help you with difficult words. When you are ready, read the passage out loud to your teacher. In your own words, tell your teacher what is happening in this passage.

B. As your teacher reads the lines in bold print out loud,* write them down. Compare your copy to the passage on this page and make corrections.

NOTE TO THE TEACHER: Spelling lists will be made of unknown words, misspelled words from dictation, and any unknown words from the word study activities. Please do not make weekly lists of more than 5 words. Keep track of words you do not cover and add them to later lists. Please keep a list of these words from week to week, noting when they are mastered.

DAY 2

A. A conjunction is a word that joins two words, or two groups of words. There are three main conjunctions: and, or, because. Point out the conjunction "and" to your teacher every place it is used in our passage.

*This is on the optional Dictation Tape.

B. Show your teacher the two ways that "and" is used: 1) to join two words, and 2) to join two groups of words. When "and" joins two words that are subjects of a sentence, the two words could be used to write two separate sentences. Here is an example:

The sentence — Bill and Bob ran to the field. — becomes these sentences:

      Bill ran to the field.   **Bob ran to the field.**

Following this example, take the first sentence in our passage and make it into two sentences.

C. The conjunction and also joins two groups or words that can make two different sentences. Here is an example:

This sentence — Dinner is ready and I am hungry. — becomes these sentences:

      Dinner is ready.   **I am hungry.**

Rewrite the first sentence in our passage into two sentences, dividing at the second conjunction and.

DAY 3

A. This story is a biography (a true story about someone's life.) Take the biographical information in this paragraph and make a time line showing Amos Fortune's life. (Use the same procedure we used in Lesson 5.)

> Amos Fortune was born in 1710 in Africa. He was captured and enslaved in 1725 at the age of 15. He was purchased at that time by the Copeland family of Boston, Massachusetts, who were a Quaker family. In 1740, Mr. Copeland died and Amos was sold to Mr. Ichabod Richardson of Woburn, Massachusetts. Amos was freed from servitude in 1769. He and Violet were married in 1779, on the day after he purchased her freedom. In 1781 he and Violet moved to Jaffrey, New Hampshire. In 1789, Amos purchased 25 acres of land, becoming a landowner. Amos Fortune died in 1801, at the age of 91.

B. Add to your time line any other important dates such as the dates of the Revolutionary War and Independence Day.

DAY 4

A. Amos and Violet were slaves for many years. Though the families that Amos lived with, the Copelands and the Richardsons, were kind to him, he was still unable to go where he pleased, or do as he pleased. In previous lessons, you have looked up the definitions of such words as liberty and freedom. Now look up the words slave and slavery. Tell your teacher what these words mean. How do you think it would feel to be a slave? Talk with your teacher about your answer.

B. Even though Amos was enslaved, he served his masters with obedience, loyalty, and service beyond what the law required of him. Why do you think Amos served his masters and their families so well? Read these scriptures with your teacher and talk about the direction the Bible gives slaves and masters: Ephesians 6:5-9; Colossians 3:22-25, 4:1.

C. Make two lists on a piece of paper, or use the page provided in the Student Activity Book. At the top of one list, write God's Directions to Slaves. At the top of the other list write God's Directions to Masters. List what each is supposed to do according to the Bible.

DAY 5

A. Listen as your teacher reads the passage you are to write from dictation.* Do not write as it is read the first time, just listen. Remember, writing from dictation is a skill you acquire with practice, like hitting a baseball. Your first attempts may not be too successful, but as you practice you will become better.

B. After you listen to the passage the second time, write what you have heard. When you have finished, compare your copy to the model.

C. Listen as your teacher dictates the spelling words you have been working on this week. Write each word as she reads it to you. After you write each word, use it in a sentence orally. When you are finished, compare your spellings to the correct spellings on your list, and make any needed corrections.

NOTE TO THE TEACHER: Be sure to add correctly spelled words to a mastery list that you keep for each student. Record the date the words are correctly spelled.

*This is on the optional Dictation Tape.

Teacher Helps:

Day 2 A.   Amos <u>and</u> Violet

peepers chimed in a marsh nearby <u>and</u> late birds called to each other

They were being helped to get going <u>and</u> the people in the land

      B.   Amos and Violet – "and" joining two words.

The other examples are "and" joining two groups of words.

Amos slept under the stars while peepers chimed in a marsh nearby.

Violet slept under the stars while peepers chimed in a marsh nearby.

      C.   Amos and Violet slept under the stars while peepers chimed in a marsh nearby. Late birds called to each other.

Day 3 A.

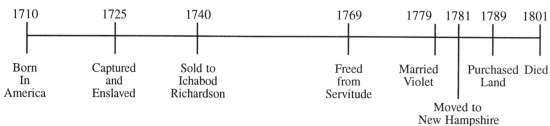

      C.   Revolutionary War - 1776–1783

Independence Day - July 4, 1776

LESSON 28

Ever since he had his freedom he had saved one small fortune and then another. Now he wanted to spend once more the hard-earned savings in the iron kettle and Violet would not let him. **What right had she to oppose him? Yet it was he who had given her freedom. The word was meaningless unless in its light each one lived up to his highest and his best.**

"Oh, Lord," Amos said, "You've always got an answer and You're always ready to give it to the man who trusts You. Keep me open-hearted this night so when it comes I'll know it's You speaking and I'll heed what You have to say."

From *Amos Fortune, Free Man* by Elizabeth Yates, cover by Lonnie Knabel. ©1950 by Elizabeth Yates McGreal, renewed ©1978 by Elizabeth Yates McGreal. Used by permission of Dutton Children's Books, a division of Penguin Books USA, Inc.

DAY 1

A. Read the passage silently. Ask your teacher to help you with difficult words. When you are ready, read the passage out loud to your teacher. In your own words, tell your teacher what is happening in this passage.

B. As your teacher reads the lines in bold print out loud,* write them down. Compare your copy to the passage on this page and make corrections.

NOTE TO THE TEACHER: Spelling lists will be made of unknown words, misspelled words from dictation, and any unknown words from the word study activities. Please do not make weekly lists of more than 5 words. Keep track of words you do not cover and add them to later lists. Keep a list of these words from week to week, noting when they are mastered. Sheets for this purpose are found in the Appendix of this book and in the Student Activity Book.

DAY 2

A. Remember our picture of base words with prefixes and suffixes? Here it is again.

The main house is the base word. The garage on the left is a

*This is on the optional Dictation Tape.

99

prefix (letters added to the beginning of a word). The extra room on the right is a suffix (letters added to the end of a word). Both prefixes and suffixes change the meaning of the base word.

Find the two words in our passage that end with -less.

B. It would seem that both have the suffix -less. The suffix -less means without. Think about the meaning of both words, thinking of them as having the suffix -less. Do both words make sense? Do both words have the suffix -less?

C. Add the suffix -less to the following words and then tell your teacher what you think they mean. Look up any words you do not know.

Make up a sentence, orally or in writing, using each word you make by adding the suffix.

> hope   home
> care   help

See if you can think of more words that have the suffix -less.

DAY 3

A. What you see in the passage can be described as a conflict, or problem. Most stories have at least one conflict, or problem which is solved in the story. In your own words, tell your teacher what you think is the conflict between Amos and Violet.

Actually, there is more to this conflict. Amos wants to spend the money to help another poor family, and Violet wants him to use it to purchase his lifelong dream of owning his own home and land. She is not trying to be selfish. She thinks Amos has been very unselfish, and wants him to see the result of all his hard work. Without looking or reading ahead, tell your teacher what you think is going to happen next.

B. There are ways that you can predict, or tell beforehand, what might happen in a story. This is called "predicting outcome." Things like what we know about a character—how they have acted before, help us predict outcome. Circumstances and events in a story also give us ideas as to what will happen next. When you are reading, stop during a story and decide what you think will happen next. Then read on and see if you were right. Compare your ending to what really happened.

C. Here are some simple circumstances. Try to predict what you think will happen next, based on what you already know.

1. It rains for days and days. The river is rising. The weather forecast calls for more rain. What could happen next? Think of more than one possibility.

2. The policeman saw a man outside a closed store. The man was looking around. The man walked over to the door knob and tried to open the door. What do you think will happen next? Think of more than one possible answer.

3. A woman and three little children are at a park. The children are playing and the woman is smiling and watching them. One of the children falls down and starts to cry. What will happen next? Think of several possible answers.

Choose one of the above situations and write a conclusion to it.

DAY 4

A. When Amos has not known what to do, or when he needed help in the past, he has often done the same thing. What does he do in this passage when faced with uncertainty about what to do? Has Amos prayed before? Look at the passage in Lesson 27.

B. By praying, Amos is saying that the final decision about what he does in his life is not up to him. Who has he left it up to? Talk with your teacher about times in her life when important decisions had to be made. How did she go about making them? Have you ever had to make decisions that were important to you? How did you make those decisions?

Think of a three or four step plan for making decisions. Write down your plan and put it where you can look at it if you need it. You may want to write it like this, using simple directions:

Step 1.
Step 2.
Step 3.
Step 4.

C. The Bible gives us a prayer that Jesus taught the disciples which asks for God's will or plan, to be done each day. Listen as your teacher reads Matthew 6:7-15. In-

101

cluded in this Scripture is a section called The Lord's Prayer. It is contained in verses 9-13. Talk with your teacher about what this prayer means. If you have not memorized the Lord's Prayer yet, this would be a good time to learn it.

The Lord's Prayer *

"Our Father who art in heaven,
Hallowed be Thy name.
Thy Kingdom come.
Thy will be done,
On earth as it is in heaven.
Give us this day our daily bread.
And forgive us our debts, as we also have forgiven our debtors.
And do not lead us into temptation,
But deliver us from evil."

* Your family may use another translation of the Bible, or say this prayer in a slightly different way.

DAY 5

A. Listen as your teacher reads the passage you are to write from dictation.* Do not write as it is read the first time, just listen. Remember, writing from dictation is a skill you acquire with practice, like hitting a baseball. Your first attempts may not be too successful, but as you practice you will become better.

B. After you listen to the passage the second time, write what you have heard. When you have finished, compare your copy to the passage at the beginning of this lesson.

C. Listen as your teacher dictates the spelling words you have been working on this week. Write each word as she reads it to you. After you write each word, use it in a sentence orally. When you are finished, compare your spellings to the correct spellings on your list, and make any needed corrections.

NOTE TO THE TEACHER: Be sure to add correctly spelled words to a master list that you keep for each student. Record the date the words are correctly spelled.

*This is on the optional Dictation Tape.

Teacher Helps:

Day 2 A. meaningless, unless

    B. No, both words would not make sense. Unless would mean "without not." Meaningless means "without meaning."

    No, only meaningless has the suffix -less. Unless is one word without a prefix or suffix.

    C. hopeless, homeless, careless, helpless

Day 3 A. Amos wants to spend the money and Violet does not.

    C. 1. The river floods its bank; the river rises to the top of the bank and the rain stops; workers come and open floodgates so the river goes down.
    2. The man tries to rob the store and gets caught, the man left his wallet inside and is worried about getting it back, the man's car won't start and he is trying to get help.
    3. The woman picks up and comforts her child, one of the other children helps the child, the child gets up and goes to the woman for comfort.

Day 4 A. He prays for God's direction to be made real to him.
    Yes, Amos has prayed before.

    B. Amos left the final decision up to God.

    Step 1. Talk to Mom and Dad.
    Step 2. Pray about it.
    Step 3. See if the Bible says anything about it.
    Step 4. Talk with Mom and Dad again, asking if my decision is all right with them.

LESSON 29

That afternoon Amos and Violet rode over to William Turner's and signed the deed that put twenty five acres of land, cleared and forest with a brook running through it, in Amos Fortune's name.

And there, by the bank of the brook, Amos built his own house—strong enough to meet the stress of time and the force of storms. He built a barn and a tanyard and excavated basins in the brook for his work.

By the end of 1789, when Amos Fortune was in his eightieth year, he became a land owner in his own right and one of his life's long dreams was fulfilled.

From *Amos Fortune, Free Man* by Elizabeth Yates, cover by Lonnie Knabel. ©1950 by Elizabeth Yates McGreal, renewed ©1978 by Elizabeth Yates McGreal. Used by permission of Dutton Children's Books, a division of Penguin Books USA, Inc.

DAY 1

A. Read the passage silently. Ask your teacher to help you with difficult words. When you are ready, read the passage out loud to your teacher. In your own words, tell your teacher what is happening in this passage.

B. As your teacher reads the lines in bold print out loud,* write them down. Compare your copy to the passage on this page and make corrections.

NOTE TO THE TEACHER: Spelling lists will be made of unknown words, misspelled words from dictation, and any unknown words from the word study activities. Please do not make weekly lists of more than 5 words. Keep track of words you do not cover and add them to later lists. Keep a list of these words from week to week, noting when they are mastered. Sheets for this purpose are found in the Appendix of this book and in the Student Activity Book.

DAY 2

A. A dictionary can give you much information about a word. Here is a sample of a dictionary entry. Read it silently as your teacher reads aloud, or you may read it aloud.

①own • ②er (ō′n③ər), ④ ⑤ ***n.*** the ⑥one who owns: *Who is the owner of this car?*

*This is on the optional Dictation Tape.

104

B. Look at the entry and tell what information is given for each number in the entry.

Look in your dictionary and find an entry for any other word. Locate the same six pieces of information that we just found. There are several keys in your dictionary that can help you. With your teacher's help, find the pronunciation key and the key to the abbreviations for the parts of speech. Talk with your teacher about these until you understand how they work.

C. Another very important piece of information about using a dictionary tells you how to find the word you want. There are words at the top of each page called "guide words." All of the words in the dictionary are in alphabetical order. Look at the guide words in order to find the page containing your word. Look through the dictionary reading some guide words. Answer these questions after looking through your dictionary.

1. What word is listed on the top left-hand corner of each page?
2. What word is listed on the upper right-hand corner of the page?
3. Would the word <u>camper</u> be on the page with these guide words—Calvin and campground?
4. Would <u>play</u> be on the page with these guide words—plastic and plausible?
5. Find the word <u>literature</u> in your dictionary. What are the guide words on that page?

DAY 3

A. Dictionaries give us more information about words than just what they mean. Use your dictionary and look up these words.

deed	bank	toward
stress	excavate	basin

Answer the following questions orally about each word:

1. What are the guide words for the page this word is on?
2. How many syllables are in this word?
3. How many meanings does this word have?
4. What does this word mean?

B. Use each of the words you looked up in a sentence, orally or in writing. Try to make up sentences that are related to the story of Amos Fortune.

C. Look through the dictionary and find five words you have never seen or heard before. Write them down in a list. Answer all the questions in part A of this activity for each word. Then make up a sentence orally using each word. You have just added five new words to your vocabulary.

DAY 4

A. This passage paints a very clear picture of the land that Amos Fortune bought from William Turner. Look back at the time line you made in Lesson 24 - Day 3. How many years did Amos work after coming to America before he was able to purchase his own home?

Amos could have purchased land sooner, had he not used his money to help others so often.

B. What does the Bible have to say about money? How do you know when you are to save your money, and when you should spend it? These are important questions we all have to think about. After reading each Scripture with your teacher, tell in your own words what you think the main point is of each Scripture.

1. Ecclesiastes 5:10
2. Malachi 3:8-10
3. Luke 6:38
4. Luke 10:7
5. Acts 20:35
6. I Timothy 6:9-10

C. Talk with your teacher about how your family decides how to spend its money, and what your family's attitudes are about money. After discussion, write a paragraph or two that tells what you believe about money and what you will do with it.

DAY 5

A. Listen as your teacher reads the passage you are to write from dictation.* Do not write as it is read the first time, just listen. Remember, writing from dictation is a skill you acquire with practice, like hitting a baseball. Your first attempts may not be too successful, but as you practice you will become better.

B. After you listen to the passage the second time, write what you have heard. When you have finished, compare your copy to the passage at the beginning of this lesson.

C. Listen as your teacher dictates the spelling words you have been working on this week. Write each word as she reads it to you. After you write each word, use it in a sentence orally. When you are finished, compare your spellings to the correct spellings on your list, and make any needed corrections.

NOTE TO THE TEACHER: Be sure to add correctly spelled words to a master list that you keep for each student. Record the date the words are correctly spelled.

Teacher Helps:

Day 2 B.   ① How to spell it, ② how many syllables it has and where to divide them, ③ how to pronounce the word, ④ what part of speech it is, ⑤ what it means, and ⑥ how to use it in a sentence.

C.   1. The first word listed on the page.
2. The last word listed on the page.
3. Yes
4. No
5. Answers will vary.

Day 4 A.   64 years.

B.   1. If you love money, you won't be satisfied with it, even if you get more.
2. God asks if we will rob Him of the tithes and offerings we owe Him. He will bless our giving.
3. However you give to others is the way blessings will be given to you.
4. A person who works is worthy to receive his wages.
5. It is more blessed to give than to receive.
6. The love of money is the root (beginning of) all kinds of evils.

*This is on the optional Dictation Tape.

LESSON 30

"Once, long years ago, I thought I could set a canoe-load of my people free by breaking the bands at my wrists and killing the white man who held the weapon. I had the strength in my hands to do such a deed and I had the fire within, but I didn't do it."

"What held you back?"

Amos shook his head. **"My hand was restrained and I'm glad that it was, for the years between have shown me that it does a man no good to be free until he knows how to live, how to walk in step with God."**

From *Amos Fortune, Free Man* by Elizabeth Yates, cover by Lonnie Knabel. ©1950 by Elizabeth Yates McGreal, renewed ©1978 by Elizabeth Yates McGreal. Used by permission of Dutton Children's Books, a division of Penguin Books USA, Inc.

DAY 1

A. Read the passage silently. Ask your teacher to help you with difficult words. When you are ready, read the passage out loud to your teacher. In your own words, tell your teacher what is happening in this passage.

B. As your teacher reads the lines in bold print out loud,* write them down. Compare your copy to the passage on this page and make corrections.

NOTE TO THE TEACHER: Spelling lists will be made of unknown words, misspelled words from dictation, and any unknown words from the word study activities. Please do not make weekly lists of more than 5 words. Keep track of words you do not cover and add them to later lists. Keep a list of these words from week to week, noting when they are mastered. Sheets for this purpose are found in the Appendix of this book and in the Student Activity Book.

DAY 2

A. Analogies show how two things relate to each other. Here is an example of an analogy. You have to figure out what kind of relationship exists between the two sets of things.

Amos Fortune : Africa   Bill Smith : America

*This is on the optional Dictation Tape.

We know that Amos was born in Africa so what do we know now about Bill Smith? See if you can tell the relationship between these words:

arm : body   wheel : car

B. Analogies are like puzzles. You have to figure out how the pieces fit together. Read these word pairs and tell your teacher the relationship between the items.

1. tree:forest   house:town
2. cub:lion   daughter:mother
3. branch:tree   tail:cat
4. day:night   dark:light
5. birds:sky   fish:water

C. Here are some incomplete analogies. Try to find out what the relationship is in the first set and fill in an appropriate word in the second set.

1. buy:sell   slave:_____
2. bird:nest   _____ :garage
3. board:fence   brick:_____
4. stars:galaxies   words:_____
5. kitten:cat   chick:_____

Try to think of at least two analogies of your own. Tell these to your teacher.

DAY 3

A. A <u>fact</u> is something that can be observed, measured, or proven to be true. Here are some examples of facts:

It is two miles from here to the store.
We had warm, sunny weather today.

Look over the passages on Amos Fortune (Lessons 27–30) and find at least three facts.

Fold a piece of paper in half vertically (as shown here by dotted line.)

Write the word "Fact" at the top left side of your paper. Under the title, make a list of the facts from Lessons 27–30. Add three facts about your family, home or hobbies.

Fact	Opinion

B. An <u>opinion</u> is a statement that tells what we think or feel about something. Here are some examples of opinions:

> I liked the book about dogs the best.
> Hamburgers taste better than hot dogs.

Reread your fact sentences. On the top of the right side of your paper write the word <u>Opinion</u>. Write an opinion (what you think or feel) to go with each fact. Here's an example:

<u>Fact</u>   <u>Opinion</u>
I play little league baseball.   Baseball is the most exciting sport.

C. Newspapers are an excellent source of facts and opinions. Together with your teacher, look through some newspaper articles for facts and opinions. Some of the words that signal opinions are: think, believe, feel, want, should. Point out at least three facts and three. Advertisements are a great source of opinions.

DAY 4

A. In the first paragraph of our passage, Amos states some facts. Reread the first paragraph, and tell your teacher the two facts he states.

In the last paragraph he tells us his opinion about not killing the men and breaking free. Reread the last paragraph and tell your teacher his opinion about not breaking free.

B. Amos did not break free when he was young, and in his old age he said that he was glad he didn't. Most people would say that to be free of a master would be the best thing. Amos doesn't seem to think that freedom at that time would have been the best for him. Why do you think he said that?

In everyone's life, there are circumstances that may seem difficult. There may be problems with making enough money, or health problems, or things like having unkind neighbors, or a house that seems too small. Thinking about what Amos said, do you think that just breaking free of every difficulty will help us the most?

C. Talk with your teacher about the way Amos responded to his masters. Can you think of a way this story could apply to your life? Discuss your answer with your teacher.

Together with your teacher, think of a situation in your life that you might want to be free of, such as chores, schoolwork, helping with brothers or sisters, etc. Write a brief description of this situation.

Discussing with your teacher, think of the things you can learn from yielding to this situation, or the benefits that can come from it. Write these down briefly. You may want to say a prayer as Amos often did, asking God to give you strength to do your job well, and a good attitude to do it. Your teacher may want to pray for you to be able to trust God to use this circumstance for your good.

DAY 5

A. Listen as your teacher reads the passage you are to write from dictation.* Do not write as it is read the first time, just listen. Remember, writing from dictation is a skill you acquire with practice, like hitting a baseball. Your first attempts may not be too successful, but as you practice you will become better.

B. After you listen to the passage the second time, write what you have heard. When you have finished, compare your copy to the passage at the beginning of this lesson.

C. Listen as your teacher dictates the spelling words you have been working on this week. Write each word as she reads it to you. After you write each word, use it in a sentence orally. When you are finished, compare your spellings to the correct spellings on your list, and make any needed corrections.

NOTE TO THE TEACHER: Be sure to add correctly spelled words to a master list that you keep for each student. Record the date the words are correctly spelled.

*This is on the optional Dictation Tape.

Teacher Helps:

Day 2 A.   Bill Smith was born in America.

An arm is a part of a body. A wheel is part of a car.

B.
1. one part of many parts that go together to make something bigger
2. younger offspring to parent
3. one part of a whole
4. opposites
5. beings and their homes

C.
1. freeman, master
2. car, truck, bike
3. house, building, wall
4. books, etc.
5. hen, rooster

Day 4 A.   He had the strength to break the bonds at his wrist and kill the white man, and he had the fire inside to do it.

He was glad that he didn't break free, because the years have taught him it would have done him no good to be free not knowing how to walk with God.

B.   He realizes that the things he learned along the way taught him much about God, about work, and about even the value of freedom.

No, we learn how to be patient, or kind, or hard working through the difficulties we face.

LESSON 31

DAY 1

A. Listen as your teacher reads the story *The Mission of John Chapman* found in the Appendix.* Then reread it silently. This story is called a folk tale, or legend.

B. Think about Johnny's life as being divided into three time periods: <u>Childhood and Youth</u> (up to 18 years old), <u>Young Explorer</u> (explorations with Nathaniel), <u>On His Own</u> (after he left Uncle Ben's.) Look over the story, and tell your teacher something about each of the three periods in John Chapman's life.

C. Now you will make some observations about the three parts of Johnny's life, and then you will write them down.

<u>Skim</u> the story. This means look over the story to remember the main ideas of each paragraph. Do not read every word. Skimming is a quick reminder of what you have read. To skim a story you have not read before, read the titles and probably the first sentence of each paragraph. This will give an idea of what the story is about.

D. Now go back and <u>scan</u> the story. This means look for specific events that go into each of the three parts mentioned in Activity B, above. Using scratch paper, make a list of three events from each part of Johnny's life that were the most interesting or exciting.

DAY 2

A. Take a piece of paper and fold into thirds like this:

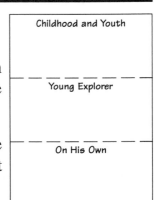

On the top part, write the heading <u>Childhood and Youth</u>. On the middle part write the heading <u>Young Explorer</u>, and on the bottom part write the heading <u>On His Own</u>.

Using the lists you developed yesterday, make up a sentence to describe each event. Write each sentence in the correct section on your divided paper.

B. When you are finished, you will have written three groups of sentences about John Chapman. Read each group of sentences aloud to your teacher and talk about any changes you could make to improve the wording.

*This is on the optional Dictation Tape.

C. Using the heading for each section, make up a sentence that tells about that part of Johnny's life. These sentences will be your topic sentences for each paragraph. Here's an example:

Childhood and Youth—Johnny Chapman had an unusual childhood and youth.

Talk with your teacher and write a sentence for each section on your paper.

DAY 3

A. Today you will tell what you think the story *The Mission of John Chapman* is about, and how you liked it. Talk with your teacher and tell what you remember when you think of the story. As you talk, tell what you think are the main points, or most important things about the story. With your teacher's help, make up three or four sentences that include the following information:

1. The title of the story.
2. Who the story is about.
3. When and where the story took place.

Your teacher may want to write the sentences for you, for you to recopy. This is the opening paragraph, or introduction of your summary report.

B. The last paragraph of your summary report will be the conclusion. Talking with your teacher, tell what you think of Johnny Chapman and what he did in his life. Write one or two sentences telling this.

Now make up one or two sentences telling whether or not you liked this story and why you felt this way.

DAY 4

A. You have now completed a summary report on the story *The Mission of John Chapman*. Try to think of a title for your report that tells about what you have written. Ask your teacher to look over your paragraphs and help you find any mistakes in punctuation or spelling. This is called proofreading.

B. After corrections have been made, recopy or type your report into its final form. This should include your name and date in the upper right hand corner.

A. You have read about and discussed the life of John Chapman. Today we will write a few sentences that tell about Johnny Chapman himself. First we will make a diagram to help us. This is called a <u>character sketch</u>. Using a piece of blank paper, write "Johnny Chapman" in the middle and draw a circle around it. Now scan your story for specific adjectives, or words that describe Johnny. Write these words around the circle as shown here. After you have finished, draw circles around each word, and attach them to the big circle with a line.

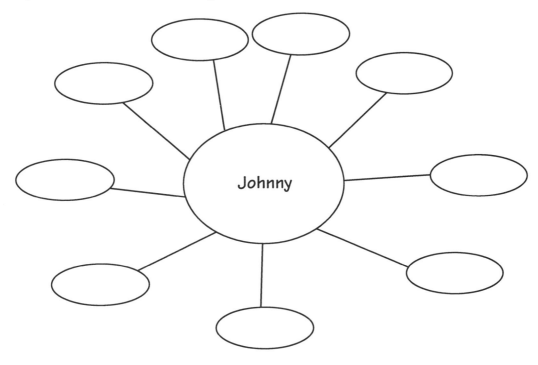

B. Read over what you have written. Talk with your teacher and see if you can think of any more words not included in the story that you think describe Johnny. Add these words to your character sketch. You could now tell about Johnny Chapman using your character sketch.

C. Using the same approach, make a character sketch that describes you. Write your name in the middle with a circle around it. Talk with your teacher and come up with a list of adjectives, or descriptions that tell about you. Try to be honest, but always be kind. Write these words around the main circle and draw circles around each word and attach them with a line to the big circle.

Take this opportunity to talk with your teacher about your strengths and weaknesses. You may want to set goals for improving some area of your life, or you may want to start thinking of ways that you can better use your strengths.

Teacher Helps:

Day 3 A.   Possible Introduction:

The title of the story is *The Mission of John Chapman.* The story is about a young boy and how he grew up. The story takes place in Massachusetts during the wilderness days.

    B.   Possible Conclusion:

I liked Johnny Chapman because he was kind and helped people and animals. I also liked the story because it shows how one person can do a great thing.

LESSONS 32 & 33

DAYS 1 & 2

Have you ever heard a speech? Maybe one your parents has given a speech, or you've heard a government official give one. During these two weeks you will prepare and present a speech of your own. There are many types of speeches and today we are going to learn three of them.

A. One type of speech is a speech which is given to inform. Listen as your teacher reads the first part of this famous speech given by Winston Churchill in 1940* (found in the Appendix). This speech was given in England before a group of government officials to tell them about a crisis that was upon the country.

The speaker continues to give facts about the situation in the country and to propose a solution. The part of the speech that you have just read is full of information about the condition of the English government. Talk to your teacher about the facts included in this speech. Do you think they are given with or without feeling? Why or why not?

B. The second type of speech is the speech given to persuade. Listen as your teacher reads a portion of a speech given 2,000 years ago* (found in the Appendix). The speech was given by Julius Caesar, a famous Roman leader, to a group of government officials called Senators.

The speaker continues by giving an example of earlier Roman leaders who did not execute their enemies and the good that came from that decision. Julius Caesar is trying to convince the Senators not to execute several men who were found guilty of a crime. Look at this portion of the speech again to see how he tries to persuade the Senators.

1. What does Julius Caesar imply is the Senators' possible difficulty in deciding this issue his way?
2. How does he try to convince them that these strong feelings will not help them make wise decisions?

In order to persuade others of his opinion, Julius Caesar presented facts to back up his opinions. He also used what he saw as his opponents' weaknesses as a basis for calling them to change their minds and follow his plan.

*This is on the optional Dictation Tape.

At the end of his speech he proposed another punishment for the criminals besides execution.

Historical note: After Julius Caesar's speech to the Senators, Marcus Porcius Cato gave a speech demanding the immediate execution of the criminals. By voicing the fears of the Senators and suggesting that Julius Caesar was merely being political, the Senate called for an immediate execution of the men without a trial. Although called a hero at first for this decision, Cato lived to regret it. He later repented the executing of Roman citizens without a trial and the deed resulted in a ruined political reputation which his enemies used against him for years.

C. The final type of speech is a speech given to demonstrate something to an audience. When you give a speech to demonstrate you show and tell your audience how to do a specific thing. Here are some examples:

How to saddle a horse.
How to throw a frisbee.
How to shoot a basketball.
How to separate an egg.
How to complete a simple craft project.

Listen as your teacher read the speech entitled *How To Open A Door*, found in the Appendix.*

Let's review the three types of speeches:
Speech to inform: gives facts and information about an event or a person.
Speech to persuade: tries to convince the audience of an opinion by giving facts to support that opinion.
Speech to demonstrate: shows and tells an audience how to do a specific thing.

DAY 3

You will now begin to prepare your own speech. Discuss with your teacher the following items to help you decide which type of speech to prepare.

1. Who will be my audience?
2. Which type of speech would be best for this audience?
3. Which type of speech would be best for me to prepare?

*This is on the optional Dictation Tape.

Once you have decided the type of speech to present, you must choose a topic for the speech.

Suggestions:

Speech to **Inform**	Speech to **Persuade**	Speech to **Demonstrate**
• Science Topic • Social Studies Topic • Family History • Bible History	• Any political/social issue • More allowance every week • Appeal for a certain vacation spot this year	• How to do any sport or baking • How to do a craft • How to draw

DAY 4 & 5

After you have decided on a topic for your speech, it is time to think about that topic. Ask yourself these questions:

1. Is the topic too big to talk about in a few minutes?
2. Can I break it down into smaller pieces?

This step in speech making is called "Narrowing Your Topic." It would be hard to make a short speech on the topic "airplanes." That topic is too big. You can, however, do a speech demonstrating how an airplane flies using a model.

When your topic is very specific, you are ready to gather the information you need for your speech.

To gather information you can:

1. Read books and magazines.
2. Talk to anyone who knows about the subject.
3. Watch a video.
4. Think about information you already know.

Make notes on notebook paper as you find the information. You can write words and phrases rather than complete sentences. Just be sure to include all the information you need—don't assume you will remember something you don't write down.

After you have collected your information, you will need to organize it in some manner. some people like to use an outline for that purpose. If you use an outline, use Roman Numerals for your main points of the speech and capital letters under each point for details. (See Lesson 22 for a review of outlines.)

    I. Main Point
        A. Detail #1
        B. Detail #2
   II. Second Main Point
        A. Detail #1
        B. Detail #2

This format may be best for a Speech to Demonstrate. Your main points can be your steps and the details will give information for each step.

If you are presenting a Speech to Inform you may create a wheel diagram such as

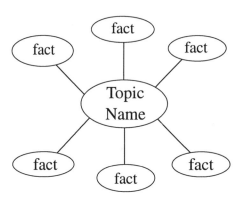

The topic is written in the center and on each spoke is information about the topic. When all your spoke circles are filled, you may want to number them for your presentation.

If you are preparing a Speech to Persuade you may use an outline with Roman Numerals as your opinions and capital letters under each opinion as facts of examples to support your opinion.

    I. Opinion
        A. Fact or example #1
        B. Fact or example #2
   II. Second Opinion
        A. Fact or example #1
        B. Fact or example #2

There are two very important parts to any speech: the beginning and the ending.

Talk to anyone you know who has given a speech and get suggestions for the beginning of your speech. Suggestions: a joke, appropriate story, question, recent incident, famous quote or verse.

The ending, or conclusion of a speech will usually call the audience to some kind of action or response. For example, if you demonstrate how to draw a cat, you may conclude by telling your audience that one day you hope they will try to draw a cat or another animal of interest. A speech on King Richard may conclude by calling the audience to read about their favorite historical figure. A speech on the increasing of an allowance may appeal to the audience to begin this new allowance rate today.

After all your information is gathered and organized, and you have your beginning and ending figured out, you are ready for your final preparations. Either write your speech, or make notes to yourself from which you will present the speech to your audience.

DAY 8 & 9

Practice giving your speech at least three times a day. You are not required to memorize the entire passage, however, you should know it well enough to be able to look up from your paper several times during the presentation.

Stand in front of a mirror as you practice. Use the following list to help you evaluate yourself. After you have practiced several times, ask your teacher or another student to evaluate you, using the list.

_____ 1. Do I read slowly?
_____ 2. Do I read clearly?
_____ 3. Do I read loud enough?
_____ 4. Am I using my voice well to communicate the meaning and feeling?
_____ 5. Am I standing up straight, but naturally?
_____ 6. Do I look at my audience enough?

DAY 10

Your presentation day has arrived, and even though you may feel nervous, you are ready for your audience because you planned for it. If you feel very nervous, ask your teacher to sit in the back of the room and give you support by smiling at you.

Teacher Helps:

Day 1 A. A new administration was formed at the request of His Majesty.

A War Cabinet was formed.

The main three party leaders will serve either on the war cabinet or in a high executive office.

The three fighting services are filled.

This speech was probably given with much feeling, because of the urgency of the situation.

B. 1. The Senators probably have strong feelings about these crimes or criminals.

2. He calls it their "duty" not to follow these emotions.
Gives his opinion that emotions only make it harder to use good judgement.
Refers to mistakes other leaders made by following their emotions.
Gives a specific example of others who did not follow their emotions.

LESSON 34

The Star-Spangled Banner
by Francis Scott Key

(Verse 1)

    O say, can you see, by the dawn's early light,

    What so proudly we hailed at the twilight's last gleaming.

    Whose broad stripes and bright stars, through the perilous fight,

    O'er the ramparts we watched were so gallantly streaming!

    And the rockets' red glare, the bombs bursting in air.

    Gave proof through the night that our flag was still there:

    O say, does that star-spangled banner yet wave

    O'er the land of the free and the home of the brave?

DAY 1

A. Listen to your teacher read the first verse of *The Star-Spangled Banner* by Francis Scott Key.* Though you may have heard this song many times, you may not have been able to understand all the words, or thought about the meaning of each phrase. Read the verse silently, pointing out unknown words to your teacher for help.

B. Carefully read this verse aloud. Try to read expressively, paying special attention to punctuation marks. Practice reading through this verse several times. Since this is a familiar verse, it should not be difficult to memorize. Work on memorizing this verse, being careful to say each word correctly. If you have a tape recorder and a blank tape, record yourself reading this verse using your most clear and expressive voice.

DAY 2

A. Either read silently, or listen as your teacher reads the excerpt from the book *Patriotic Songs, Color the Classics* series, entitled *The Star-Spangled Banner* from the Appendix.* After reading this, talk with your teacher about the events described. Make a list of these events. You do not need to use sentences for your list. You may use phrases. You may want to color the picture of the bombardment of Ft. McHenry, also found in the Appendix.

*This is on the optional Dictation Tape.

B. The first verse of *The Star-Spangled Banner* is full of interesting words, images and thoughts. The colorful language in this verse helps us feel like we were there at Fort McHenry. Read over this list of words. Look up their definitions. Find the meaning that is used in the passage.

hailed	rampart	gleaming	gallantly	rocket
bomb	spangled	banner	perilous	glare

C. Reread the first verse of *The Star-Spangled Banner* silently. Make a list of any other words that are new or whose meaning is unknown to you. Look these words up in the dictionary, and tell your teacher what they mean.

DAY 3

A. The bombardment of Ft. McHenry was part of what is known as the War of 1812. Using an encyclopedia, or other reference book on history, look up the War of 1812.

B. After reading, answer these questions orally during discussion with your teacher.

1. How long did this war last, and where did it take place?
2. What issues were being fought over during the War of 1812?
3. What effect did this war have on America?
4. Who won the war?

C. Here are some terms that became widely used relating to the War of 1812. Look them up in the dictionary and tell your teacher their meanings and the roles they played in the war:

impressment
frigate
privateer

DAY 4

You have read about and discussed the War of 1812. You have also read a brief telling of Francis Scott Key's story about the writing of *The Star-Spangled Banner*. Reread the ninth paragraph of the story about *The Star-Spangled Banner* that begins with the sentence, "By early morning..." from the Appendix. Imagine that you are witnessing this scene, like the people in the illustration. Write a paragraph telling how you would feel, if you had been there. It doesn't have to be written in the same style as the paragraph, but use the same events in your paragraph. They are:

1. Morning has come.
2. You look at the fort.
3. You see the American flag still waving.

DAY 5

One of the most important things a writer does to make poetry special is to create imagery for us. An image consists of words that make us see pictures in our minds. Along with the picture, the poet might also provide something to hear, taste, smell, or feel. Images are the special effects of poetry. They help us understand the poem by helping us experience it.

Make two lists of images from verse one of *The Star-Spangled Banner*.

A. First, list all the words and phrases you can find that describe the battle.

B. Secondly, list all the words and phrases that describe our flag.

C. Look, again, at the images describing the battle scene. Describe the whole battle as best you can by concentrating on the images.

NOTE TO THE TEACHER: If your student can't think of anything, try a few of the leading questions in the Teacher Helps section, especially question #8.

Teacher Helps:

Day 3 B.
1. War was declared by the United States in June, 1812 and the Treaty of Gent was signed in December, 1814. It was fought in America, around the Great Lakes and the Northeast, and on the waterways.
2. The British and French were already at war, and the Americans wanted to maintain trade, but people wanted to side with one country or the other. There also was the desire to acquire land in the North American continent from these countries. All of these factors led to war.
3. The war served to distance Americans from their European ties, to show the need for a strong military, and to reinforce the idea that it was not good to become entangled in foreign affairs. It also seemed that negotiation was a better way to settle issues than war.
4. When the Treaty of Gent was signed no one really won; however, America remained independent of European nations and developed friendly ties.

Day 5 A.   perilous fight, ramparts, rockets' red glare, bombs bursting in air.

B.   broad stripes, bright stars, gallantly streaming, star-spangled banner, wave.

C.
1. Describe the ramparts.
2. How did the American soldiers feel behind those ramparts?
3. Where were the British?
4. What weapons did the British have for firing rockets and bombs?
5. Could the bombs go over the ramparts into the fort? What makes you think so?
6. Did the British have many bombs, or just a few?
7. Why was it such a perilous fight?
8. In addition to what they saw, what did the soldiers hear, smell, taste, feel?

LESSON 35

(Verse 4)
> O thus be it ever, when freemen shall stand
> Between their loved homes and the war's desolation!
> Blest with victory and peace, may the heaven-rescued land
> Praise the Power that hath made and preserved us a nation.
> Then conquer we must, when our cause it is just,
> And this be our motto: "In God is our trust,"
> And the star-spangled banner in triumph shall wave
> O'er the land of the free and the home of the brave!

DAY 1

A. Listen as your teacher reads the fourth verse of *The Star-Spangled Banner* by Francis Scott Key* After listening, read the verse silently. Point out any new words, or words with unknown meanings. Make a list of these words.

B. Carefully read this verse aloud. Try to read it expressively, paying special attention to punctuation marks. Practice reading through this verse several times and begin to memorize it. (For review of how to memorize, reread Lesson 1, Day 5.)

C. Look up the definitions of the words on your list from activity A, above. Make up a sentence, orally or in writing, using each of the words you defined. Make sure you understand the meaning of words such as desolation, preserved, cause, and motto.

DAY 2

A. When someone writes a poem, he has a message that he wants you to understand. We call this the "content" of the poem.

Look at verse four of *The Star-Spangled Banner.* Look up any words that you don't know, if you haven't already done so. This is the first step toward understanding a poem's content.

B. Sometimes it is helpful to read the poem very slowly and carefully, getting the meaning a little at a time. In your own words, orally or in writing, explain what verse four says by examining the following parts.

*This is on the optional Dictation Tape.

127

1. What do the first two lines mean to you?

2. What do lines three and four tell us?

3. What does line five say, and what does line six add to the meaning of line five?

4. Lines seven and eight make the conclusion that our nation can be free if our attitude toward God is right. What three things does verse four tell us to have in our attitude toward God?

C. Write a short paragraph summarizing the content of verse four of *The Star-Spangled Banner.*

DAYS 3 & 4

A. An essay is something you write to explain a point of view (an opinion), to report information or to challenge people's thinking. Your assignment is to write an essay. You may write one entitled *Why I Am Glad to be an American.* This would be considered a "personal essay." Or, you may write an essay to report information, entitled *What I Have Learned about America.* To begin, reread the patriotic poems contained in this book and any notes or paragraphs you have written about America.

B. Talk with your teacher about your topic for the essay. Ask yourself questions such as "Why am I glad to be an American?" or "What did I learn about America?" Answer each question with at least three responses. Make a list of your answers.

C. Each one of the answers on your list will become a topic sentence for a paragraph in your essay. Using a piece of paper for each answer on your list, write one topic sentence on each piece of paper. Remember, a topic sentence is a sentence which tells the most important thing about the paragraph.

D. Under each topic sentence write two or three sentences giving details of your topic sentence or reasons why your topic sentence is true. You have now written paragraphs. These paragraphs will make up the body of your essay.

E. The introduction to your essay should tell your reader what the essay is about and capture your reader's attention so he will want to read the rest of your paper. Write this introductory paragraph in three or more sentences on a separate piece of paper.

F. Your closing paragraph will connect the main points of the body of your essay. This conclusion will also tell your reader why it was important for you to write this essay.

On a separate piece of paper write three or more sentences concluding your essay.

G. At this point you should have at least five different pieces of paper. Put them in order with the introductory paragraph first, the body paragraphs next, and the closing paragraph last. This is the rough draft of your essay. Reread it and edit your writing as needed. Ask your teacher for help.

H. When you are satisfied with your writing, recopy or type the final version of your essay. Be sure the paragraphs are in the correct order, and write them on one or two pieces of paper. Reread your final copy to correct any mistakes in your rewriting.

DAY 5

Present your essay to your family or audience. You may also want to present dramatic readings of other stories or poems, presentations from memory or songs concerning America. There are many ways to make this presentation a special event—such as inviting other family members to contribute, making and serving refreshments, videotaping this presentation, or including drama.

Teacher Helps:

Day 2 B.
1. We must go to war so that another country—in this case, England—can't take away our freedom.
2. If we win the war we'll have the blessing of peace, and we will preserve our nation. However, we mustn't forget that God is the one who grants us the victory.
3. If we are fighting for the right reasons, then we must do all we can to win. Line six adds that we should always trust in God.
4. We must believe that God is having us fight for a cause that is just. We must trust in Him. We must thank Him for the victory.

STUDENT
EDITING MODELS

1

America
by Samuel Francis Smith (1808-1895)

My country, 'tis of thee.
Sweet land of liberty,
Of thee I sing;
Land where my fathers died,
Land of the Pilgrims' pride,
From every mountain side
Let Freedom ring.

2

(verse 4)

Our fathers' God, to Thee,
Author of liberty,
To Thee we sing;
Long may our land be bright
With Freedom's holy light;
Protect us by Thy might,
Great God, our King.

3

Mr. Poppers Penguins
by Richard & Florence Atwater

Next day the picture of Mr. Popper and Captain Cook appeared in the Stillwater *Morning Chronicle*, with a paragraph about the house painter who had received a penguin by air express from Admiral Drake in the faraway Antarctic. Then the Associated Press picked up the story, and a week later the photograph, in rotogravure, could be seen in the Sunday edition of the most important newspapers in all the large cities in the country.

Naturally, the Poppers all felt very proud and happy.

From *Mr. Popper's Penguins* by Richard and Florence Atwater. Copyright ©1938 by Florence Atwater and Richard Atwater; © renewed 1966 by Florence Atwater, Doris Atwater, and Carroll Atwater Bishop. By permission of Little, Brown and Company.

4

Captain Cook was not happy, however. He had suddenly ceased his gay, exploring little walks about the house, and would sit most of the day, sulking, in the refrigerator. Mr. Popper had removed all the stranger objects, leaving only the marbles and checkers, so that Captain Cook now had a nice, orderly little rookery...

"Better leave him alone, children," said Mrs. Popper. "He feels mopey, I guess."

From *Mr. Popper's Penguins* by Richard and Florence Atwater. Copyright ©1938 by Florence Atwater and Richard Atwater; © renewed 1966 by Florence Atwater, Doris Atwater, and Carroll Atwater Bishop. By permission of Little, Brown and Company.

5

But it was soon clear that it was something worse than mopiness that ailed Captain Cook. All day he would sit with his little white-circled eyes staring out sadly from the refrigerator. His coat had lost its lovely, glossy look; his round little stomach grew flatter each day.

He would turn away now when Mrs. Popper would offer him some canned shrimps.

From *Mr. Popper's Penguins* by Richard and Florence Atwater. Copyright ©1938 by Florence Atwater and Richard Atwater; © renewed 1966 by Florence Atwater, Doris Atwater, and Carroll Atwater Bishop. By permission of Little, Brown and Company.

6

That night the Poppers sat up all night, taking turns changing the ice packs.

It was no use. In the morning Mrs. Popper took Captain Cook's temperature again. It had gone up to one hundred and five.

Everyone was sympathetic. The reporter on the *Morning Chronicle* stopped in to inquire about the penguin. The neighbors brought in all sorts of broths and jellies to try to tempt the little fellow. Even Mrs. Callahan, who had never had a very high opinion of Captain Cook, made a lovely frozen custard for him. Nothing did any good. Captain Cook was too far gone.

From *Mr. Popper's Penguins* by Richard and Florence Atwater. Copyright ©1938 by Florence Atwater and Richard Atwater; © renewed 1966 by Florence Atwater, Doris Atwater, and Carroll Atwater Bishop. By permission of Little, Brown and Company.

7

Surely if anyone anywhere had any idea what could cure a dying penguin, this man would.

Two days later there was an answer from the Curator... "Perhaps you do not know that we too have, in our aquarium at Mammoth City, a penguin from the Antarctic. It is failing rapidly, in spite of everything we have done for it. **I have wondered lately whether it is not suffering from loneliness. Perhaps that is what ails your Captain Cook. I am, therefore, shipping you, under separate cover, our penguin.** You may keep her."

And that is how Greta came to live at 432 Proudfoot Avenue.

From *Mr. Popper's Penguins* by Richard and Florence Atwater. Copyright ©1938 by Florence Atwater and Richard Atwater; © renewed 1966 by Florence Atwater, Doris Atwater, and Carroll Atwater Bishop. By permission of Little, Brown and Company.

12

The Trumpet of the Swan
by E.B. White

"Well," said the cob, "I guess it's no use. I guess you are dumb."

When he heard the word "dumb," Louis felt like crying. The cob saw that he had hurt Louis' feelings. "You misunderstand me, my son," he said in a comforting voice. "You failed to understand my use of the word 'dumb,' which has two meanings. If I had called you a dumb cluck or a dumb bunny, that would have meant that I had a poor opinion of your intelligence. Actually, I think you are perhaps the brightest, smartest, most intelligent of all my cygnets. Words sometimes have two meanings; the word 'dumb' is such a word. ...A person who can't speak is called dumb. That simply means he can't say anything. Do you understand?"

The Trumpet of the Swan by E.B. White. Text ©1970 by E.B. White. Selection reprinted by permission of HarperCollins Publishers.

13

"Do not let an unnatural sadness settle over you, Louis," said the cob. "Swans must be cheerful, not sad; graceful, not awkward; brave, not cowardly. **Remember that the world is full of youngsters who have some sort of handicap that they must overcome.** *You* **apparently have a speech defect. I am sure you will overcome it, in time.** There may even be some slight advantage, at your age, in not being able to say anything. It compels you to be a good listener. The world is full of talkers, but it is rare to find anyone who listens."

The Trumpet of the Swan by E.B. White. Text ©1970 by E.B. White. Selection reprinted by permission of HarperCollins Publishers.

14

"There are mechanical devices that convert air into beautiful sounds. One such device is called a trumpet. I saw a trumpet once, in my travels. **I think you may need a trumpet in order to live a full life. I've *never known* a Trumpeter Swan to need a trumpet, but your case is different. I intend to get you what you need.** I don't know how I will manage this, but in the fullness of time it shall be accomplished. And now that our talk has come to a close, let us return gracefully to the other end of the pond, where your mother and your brothers and sisters await us!"

The Trumpet of the Swan by E.B. White. Text ©1970 by E.B. White.
Selection reprinted by permission of HarperCollins Publishers.

15

The cob turned and swam off. Louis followed. It had been an unhappy morning for him. He felt frightened at being different from his brothers and sisters. It scared him to be different. He couldn't understand why he had come into the world without a voice. Everyone else seemed to have a voice. Why didn't he? "Fate is cruel," he thought. "Fate is cruel to me." Then he remembered that his father had promised to help, and he felt better.

The Trumpet of the Swan by E.B. White. Text ©1970 by E.B. White.
Selection reprinted by permission of HarperCollins Publishers.

16

America, the Beautiful
by Katherine Lee Bates (1859-1929)

O beautiful for spacious skies.
For amber waves of grain.
For purple mountain majesties
Above the fruited plain!
America! America!
God shed His grace on thee
And crown thy good with brotherhood
From sea to shining sea!

17

David Livingstone – Foe of Darkness
by Jeannette Eaton

Altogether different was the reception given him a week later by
an important chief. **This native was enchanted to see a white
man and very curious to know what brought him to a section where only traders had ever come.** David told him of his
mission and the chief begged to learn about the white man's
God.

Text excerpt, pg. 52 from *David Livingstone - Foe of Darkness,* by Jeannette
Eaton. Copyright © 1947 by William Morrow & Company, Inc. By permission
of William Morrow & Company, Inc.

18

One afternoon David sat with him under a great baobab tree. The chief was full of praise for the English doctor's skill in curing a young tribesman of a badly infected wound.

Then suddenly the chief flung out both his hands in passionate entreaty. "I wish you would change my heart. Give me medicine to change it, for it is proud and angry, angry always."

Text excerpt, pg. 52 from *David Livingstone - Foe of Darkness,* by Jeannette Eaton. Copyright © 1947 by William Morrow & Company, Inc. By permission of William Morrow & Company, Inc.

19

Looking into the glowing dark eyes, David said gently, "If you will let the loving spirit of Christ enter your heart, it will be changed."

"Nay!" cried the chief and beat his breast with both hands. "I wish to have it changed by medicine and to have it changed at once, for it is always very proud and very uneasy and continually angry with someone."

Text excerpt, pg. 52 from *David Livingstone - Foe of Darkness,* by Jeannette Eaton. Copyright © 1947 by William Morrow & Company, Inc. By permission of William Morrow & Company, Inc.

20

David smiled pityingly at this very human wish for a quick dose of holiness. "Alas, medicine heals only the body. Love, a thing of the spirit, must push anger from your heart."

Text excerpt, pg. 52 from *David Livingstone - Foe of Darkness,* by Jeannette Eaton. Copyright © 1947 by William Morrow & Company, Inc. By permission of William Morrow & Company, Inc.

23

Strawberry Girl
by Lois Lenski

Mr. Boyer had sent word to all the neighbors that he was grinding cane. People began to drop in—the Tatums, the Cooks and others. The men went to the field where they cut the long cane stalks and hauled them in. They took turns feeding the stalks into the rollers. Cane pulp, called "pummy" fell to the ground at one side.

The pale green milky-looking cane juice poured out slowly into a barrel on the other side. Flies began to come, attracted by its sweetness. Like the flies, children and grown-ups came too, <u>all</u> eager to taste.

Selection reprinted from *Strawberry Girl* ©1945 by permission of the Lois Lenski Covey Foundation, Inc.

24

She found Dovey and took the three little girls to a shady spot under the big umbrella tree. She made play dollies out of towels for them. She brought sugar cane, peeled it down and gave them pieces to suck and chew. She promised them candy at the candy-pulling in the evening.

With a piece of sugar cane in her mouth, she ran back to the mill. Semina was still making her obedient rounds. The mule walked with her eyes closed as if she could go on forever.

Selection reprinted from *Strawberry Girl* ©1945
by permission of the Lois Lenski Covey Foundation, Inc.

25

At dusk-dark the real fun began.

Sam Slater and Gus and Joe appeared. No frolic was complete without them. Sam brought his fiddle into the house and struck up a lively tune, while Shoestring stood at his side and picked on the violin strings with knitting needles, for an accompaniment. **The men and women formed into lines and Sam Slater called the dance steps in a loud voice. Soon the rooms and porches were a flurry of movement, music and laughter.** Joe Slater danced fancy steps, and made the people laugh. "He shore can cut the fool!" they said.

Selection reprinted from *Strawberry Girl* ©1945
by permission of the Lois Lenski Covey Foundation, Inc.

26

Meanwhile Mr. Boyer had set fire to a pine stump near by. **When darkness came down, he had a great bonfire burning to light up the yard. The boys ran to pile on more lightwood knots whenever it burned low. It hissed and crackled and popped, bathing the dancing figures in a pattern of light and shadow.**

Mr. Boyer made the candy himself. He boiled the syrup down to just the right temperature, then poured the thickening mixture out on many plates to cool.

Birdie took plates to the little Slater girls and Dovey and showed them how to pull.

Selection reprinted from *Strawberry Girl* ©1945
by permission of the Lois Lenski Covey Foundation, Inc.

27

Amos Fortune, Free Man
by Elizabeth Yates

Amos and Violet slept under the stars while peepers chimed in a marsh nearby and late birds called to each other. **They were free. They were starting life anew. They were being helped to get going and the people in the land to which they had come were showing gladness at their arrival.**

"God give me strength for many years to do my work well," Amos prayed in the quiet of his heart.

From *Amos Fortune, Free Man* by Elizabeth Yates, cover by Lonnie Knabel. ©1950
by Elizabeth Yates McGreal, renewed ©1978 by Elizabeth Yates McGreal. Used by
permission of Dutton Children's Books, a division of Penguin Books USA, Inc.

28

Ever since he had his freedom he had saved one small fortune and then another. Now he wanted to spend once more the hard-earned savings in the iron kettle and Violet would not let him. **What right had she to oppose him? Yet it was he who had given her freedom. The word was meaningless unless in its light each one lived up to his highest and his best.**

"Oh, Lord," Amos said, "You've always got an answer and You're always ready to give it to the man who trusts You. Keep me open-hearted this night so when it comes I'll know it's You speaking and I'll heed what You have to say."

From *Amos Fortune, Free Man* by Elizabeth Yates, cover by Lonnie Knabel. ©1950 by Elizabeth Yates McGreal, renewed ©1978 by Elizabeth Yates McGreal. Used by permission of Dutton Children's Books, a division of Penguin Books USA, Inc.

29

That afternoon Amos and Violet rode over to William Turner's and signed the deed that put twenty five acres of land, cleared and forest with a brook running through it, in Amos Fortune's name.

And there, by the bank of the brook, Amos built his own house—strong enough to meet the stress of time and the force of storms. He built a barn and a tanyard and excavated basins in the brook for his work.

By the end of 1789, when Amos Fortune was in his eightieth year, he became a land owner in his own right and one of his life's long dreams was fulfilled.

From *Amos Fortune, Free Man* by Elizabeth Yates, cover by Lonnie Knabel. ©1950 by Elizabeth Yates McGreal, renewed ©1978 by Elizabeth Yates McGreal. Used by permission of Dutton Children's Books, a division of Penguin Books USA, Inc.

30

"Once, long years ago, I thought I could set a canoe-load of my people free by breaking the bands at my wrists and killing the white man who held the weapon. I had the strength in my hands to do such a deed and I had the fire within, but I didn't do it."

"What held you back?"

Amos shook his head. **"My hand was restrained and I'm glad that it was, for the years between have shown me that it does a man no good to be free until he knows how to live, how to walk in step with God."**

From *Amos Fortune, Free Man* by Elizabeth Yates, cover by Lonnie Knabel. ©1950 by Elizabeth Yates McGreal, renewed ©1978 by Elizabeth Yates McGreal. Used by permission of Dutton Children's Books, a division of Penguin Books USA, Inc.

34

The Star-Spangled Banner
by Francis Scott Key

(Verse 1)
O say, can you see, by the dawn's early light,
What so proudly we hailed at the twilight's last gleaming.
Whose broad stripes and bright stars, through the perilous fight,
O'er the ramparts we watched were so gallantly streaming!
And the rockets' red glare, the bombs bursting in air,
Gave proof through the night that our flag was still there:
O say, does that star-spangled banner yet wave
O'er the land of the free and the home of the brave?

35

(Verse 4)

O thus be it ever, when freemen shall stand
Between their loved homes and the war's desolation!
Blest with victory and peace, may the heaven-rescued land
Praise the Power that hath made and preserved us a nation.
Then conquer we must, when our cause it is just,
And this be our motto: "In God is our trust,"
And the star-spangled banner in triumph shall wave
O'er the land of the free and the home of the brave!

APPENDIX

Spelling Journal for_____

Teacher's Use	Word For Study	Date Added to List	Date Mastered
✔	**appear**	3/6/94	4/12/94

These Spelling Journal sheets are referenced in several lessons throughout this book and are provided for your convenience. Permission is granted by Common Sense Press to photocopy these two pages for use with this book.

Spelling Journal for_____

Teacher's Use	Word For Study	Date Added to List	Date Mastered

These Spelling Journal sheets are referenced in several lessons throughout this book and are provided for your convenience.
Permission is granted by Common Sense Press to photocopy these two pages for use with this book.

Lesson 1 - Day 4

Used by permission from *Color the Patriotic Classics.* One in the series of historical books and musical cassette tapes from *Color the Classics* by Carmen Ziarkowski.

America
(My Country, 'Tis of Thee)
Samuel Francis Smith 1808-1895

Samuel Francis Smith was born in Boston, Massachusetts on October 21,1808. He was an only child who developed a fascination with the patriotic history of our country.

One spring morning in 1815, the pastor of *Christ Church* began his sermon discussing the events of *Paul Revere's ride to Lexington.* Samuel often daydreamed about that heroic horse ride. He wondered what it would have been like to have traveled all those miles through the middle of the night. How did the British find out about Lexington? What was Paul Revere thinking as he crossed the Charles River? How fast was he riding? How long did it take him to get all the way to Lexington? Would he be caught? Would he ever see his family again? Oh, how Samuel wished he could have been there!

One day while waiting for his school friends, he happened to see the church maintenance man, Mr. Perry, sweeping the steps of Christ Church. Samuel asked him if he saw Paul Revere anymore. Perry mentioned that Paul was quite old now and that only his son, Joseph Revere, came to church. They sat and talked about the event that followed the hanging of the *two lanterns.* Perry described how Paul had to sneak past the British warship, the Somerset, in the channel and mount the horse that was waiting for him on the other side. Then Mr. Perry pulled out a set of old keys and said, "Come with me." Curiously, the boy followed the custodian up the stairs to the belfry. After opening the door, The two stood there looking at two old lanterns. One was broken. Samuel's eyes could not have widened any bigger. *"Are these...?"* *"Yes,"* said Mr. Perry, *"they certainly are!"*

Samuel's father had one dream for his only son. He wanted Samuel to attend *Harvard University* and receive a great education. Harvard was founded by men from England's University of Oxford and University of Cambridge. These Puritan men and their families believed that England's Universities were corrupt. Their intent was to establish a University in America with moral character, dependence upon scriptural principles and high

150

academic standards. For many years, Mr. Smith, worked hard to make sure his son could attend that University. Eventually, his long hours as a *cooper* took their toll. When Samuel was 15, his father died unexpectedly. It was time to take care of his mother and fulfill his father's dream. Within a short time, Samuel was studying diligently at Harvard where he made many friends. *Oliver Wendell Holmes* and *Lowell Mason* were among his closest lifelong friends. Samuel quickly earned a reputation as a linguist and a writer. He translated and wrote for many newspapers and journals. Because he studied all day and all night, he eventually mastered Latin, Greek, German, as well as 11 other languages.

He graduated form Harvard in 1829. Samuel was asked by many what he was going to do with his life after college. He considered law, medicine, teaching and translating. After much prayer, he decided to enroll in *Andover Theological Seminary* to become a pastor.

In February of 1831, his first year at Andover, 24 year-old Samuel heard a loud knock on his door. There stood Lowell Mason, a popular musician, with an arm full of books. Lowell, who did not understand German, asked Smith to translate the music books from German to English. Lowell was looking for an appropriate piece of music that he could use with the children for the upcoming 4th of July celebration five months away. Samuel accepted the task and Lowell left.

Samuel came across a piece of music that instantly grabbed his attention. He took a scrap of paper from the wastepaper basket and quickly jotted down 5 stanzas in 30 minutes. Thinking he had better continue with the work that Lowell had just left him, he placed the wastepaper in one of the books and forgot all about it. Little did he realize that the words he adapted to the tune would become a national hymn and that the tune would be shared by both England (*God Save the King*) and America.

On July 4th of that same year, Samuel walked down to the annual celebration given by the children of the community. What a shock to see the children stand up, follow the music leader, Lowell Mason, and sing the 5 verses that he had completely forgotten. "*My verses*," he exclaimed. After the performance was over, the applause was overwhelming. Even more thrilling was the young woman, *Mary White Smith*, who came up to congratulate him for such a beautiful poem. She later became Mrs. Samuel Smith.

Samuel preached in several large Baptist churches for many years. He composed over 150 hymns during his lifetime. Samuel always had a love for missions; he strongly promoted them. One of his sons became a missionary to Burma. When all his children were grown, he and Mary visited many countries as missionaries.

Annual Celebrations: Lowell wanted Smith to pick a melody from the collection of books and translate the German into English for the children's celebration. It was performed in Boston on July 4, 1831 at the Park Street Church. Smith did not know he was using God Save the King. He was later accused of being pro-British. It became so popular that the tune was sung at patriotic rallies, schools and during the Civil War. One reason for its success was because people already knew the tune. There were originally 5 stanzas but the last one was dropped because of its anti-British sentiment. The present 4 stanzas are exactly the way he wrote them. No revisions. The song was translated into Swedish, Latin, Italian and German. Once it became popular with the Americans, Samuel commented, "If only I had known that my song would be so well liked, I would have taken greater pains with it."

Lesson 2 - Day 1 B.

Amendment 1

Congress shall make no law respecting an establishment of religion, or prohibiting the free exercise thereof; or abridging the freedom of speech, or of the press; or the right of the people peaceable to assemble, and to petition the government for a redress of grievance.

Amendment 2

A well-regulated militia being necessary to the security of a free State, the right of the people to keep and bear arms shall not be infringed.

Amendment 3

No soldier shall, in time of peace, be quartered in any house without the consent of the owner; nor in time of war but in a manner to be prescribed by law.

Amendment 4

The right of the people to be secure in their persons, houses, papers and effects, against unreasonable searches and seizures, shall not be violated, and no warrants shall issue but upon probable cause, supported by oath or affirmation, and particularly describing the place to be searched, and the persons or things to be seized.

Amendment 5

No person shall be held to answer for a capital or otherwise infamous crime, unless on a presentment or indictment of a grand jury, except in cases arising in the land or naval forces, in the militia, when in actual service in time of war or public danger; nor shall any person be subject for the same offense to be twice put in jeopardy of life or limb; nor shall be compelled in any criminal case to be a witness against himself, nor be deprived of life, liberty, or property, without due process of law; nor shall private property be taken for public use, without just compensation.

Amendment 6

In all criminal prosecutions the accused shall enjoy the right to a speedy and public trial, by an impartial jury of the State and district wherein the crime shall have been committed, which district shall have been previously ascertained by law, and to be informed to the nature and cause of the accusation; to be confronted with the witnesses against him; to have compulsory process for obtaining witnesses in his favor and to have the assistance of counsel for his defense.

Amendment 7

In suits at common law, where the value in controversy shall exceed twenty dollars, the right of trial by jury shall be preserved, and no fact tried by a jury shall be otherwise reexamined in any court of the United States than according to the rules of the common law.

Amendment 8

Excessive bail shall not be required, nor excessive fines imposed, nor cruel and unusual punishments inflicted.

Amendment 9

The enumeration in the Constitution of certain rights shall not be construed to deny or disparage others retained by the people.

Amendment 10

The powers not delegated to the United States by the Constitution, nor prohibited by it to the States, are reserved to the States respectively, or to the people.

Paul Revere's Ride
Henry Wadsworth Longfellow

Listen, my children, and you shall hear
Of the midnight ride of Paul Revere,
On the eighteenth of April, in Seventy-five;
Hardly a man is now alive
Who remembers that famous day and year.

He said to his friend, "If the British march
By land or sea from the town tonight,
Hang a lantern aloft in the belfry arch
Of the North Church tower as a signal light,–

One, if by land, and two, if by sea;
And I on the opposite shore will be,
Ready to ride and spread the alarm
Through every Middlesex village and farm,
For the country folk to be up and to arm."

Then he said, "Good night!" and with muffled oar
Silently rowed to the Charlestown shore,
Just as the moon rose over the bay,
Where swinging wide at her moorings lay
The Somerset, British man-of-war;
A phantom ship, with each mast and spar
Across the moon like a prison bar,
And a huge black hulk, that was magnified
By its own reflection in the tide.

Meanwhile, his friend, through alley and street,
Wanders and watched with eager ears,
Till in the silence around him he hears
The muster of men at the barrack door,
The sound of arms, and the tramp of feet,
And the measured tread of the grenadiers,
Marching down to their boats on the shore.

Then he climbed the tower of the Old North Church,
By the wooden stairs, with stealthy tread,
To the belfry-chamber overhead,
And startled the pigeons from their perch
On the somber rafters, that round him made
Masses and moving shapes of shade,–
By the trembling ladder, steep and tall,
To the highest window in the wall,
Where he paused to listen and look down
A moment on the roofs of the town,
And the moonlight flowing over all.

Beneath, in the churchyard, lay the dead,
In their night-encampment on the hill,
Wrapped in silence so deep and still
That he could hear, like a sentinel's tread,
The watchful night-wind, as it went
Creeping along from tent to tent,
And seeming to whisper, "All is well!"
A moment only he feels the spell
Of the place and the hour, and the secret dread
Of the lonely belfry and the dead;
For suddenly all his thoughts are bent
On a shadowy something far away,
Where the river widens to meet the bay,–
A line of black that bends and floats
On the rising tide, like a bridge of boats.

Meanwhile, impatient to mount and ride,
Booted and spurred, with a heavy stride
On the opposite shore walked Paul Revere.
Now he patted his horse's side,
Now gazed at the landscape far and near,
Then, impetuous, stamped the earth,
And turned and tightened his saddle-girth;
But mostly he watched with eager search
The belfry-tower of the Old North Church,
As it rose above the graves on the hill,
Lonely and spectral and somber and still.
And lo! as he looks, on the belfry's height

A glimmer, and then a gleam of light!
He springs to the saddle, the bridle he turns,
But lingers and gazes, till full on his sight
A second lamp in the belfry burns!

A hurry of hoofs in a village street,
A shape in the moonlight, a bulk in the dark,
And beneath, from the pebbles, in passing, a spark
Struck out by a steed flying fearless and fleet;
That was all! And yet, through the gloom and the light
The fate of a nation was riding that night;
And the spark struck out by that steed in his flight,
Kindled the land into flame with his heat.

He has left the village and mounted the steep,
And beneath him, tranquil and broad and deep,
Is the Mystic, meeting the ocean tides;
And under the alders, that skirt its edge,
Now soft on the sand, now loud on the ledge,
Is heard the tramp of his steed as he rides.

It was twelve by the village clock
When he crossed the bridge into Medford town.
He heard the crowing of the cock,
And the barking of the farmer's dog,
And felt the damp of the river fog,
That rises after the sun goes down.

It was one by the village clock,
When he galloped into Lexington.
He saw the gilded weathercock
Swim in the moonlight as he passed,
And the meeting-house windows, blank and bare,
Gaze at him with a spectral glare,
As if they already stood aghast
At the bloody work they would look upon.

It was two by the village clock,
When he came to the bridge in Concord town.
He heard the bleating of the flock,

And the twitter of birds among the trees,
And felt the breath of the morning breeze
Blowing over the meadows brown.
And one was safe and asleep in his bed
Who at the bridge would be first to fall,
Who that day would be lying dead,
Pierced by a British musket-ball.

You know the rest. In the books you have read,
How the British Regulars fired and fled,–
How the farmers gave them ball for ball,
From behind each fence and farmyard wall,
Chasing the redcoats down the lane,
Then crossing the fields to emerge again
Under the trees at the turn of the road,
And only pausing to fire and load.
So through the night rode Paul Revere;
And so through the night went his cry of alarm
To every Middlesex village and farm,–
A cry of defiance, and not of fear,
A voice in the darkness, a knock at the door,
And a word that shall echo forevermore!
For, borne on the night-wind of the Past,
Through all our history, to the last,
In the hour of darkness and peril and need,
The people will waken and listen to hear
The hurrying hoofbeats of that steed,
And the midnight message of Paul Revere.

Used by permission from *Color the Patriotic Classics.* One in the series of historical books and
musical cassette tapes from *Color the Classics* by Carmen Ziarkowski.

159

America
by Samuel Francis Smith

My country, 'tis of thee,
sweet land of liberty,
Of thee I sing:
Land where my fathers died,
Land of the pilgrims' pride,
From every mountain side
let freedom ring!

My native country, thee,
land of the noble free,
Thy name I love:
I love thy rocks and rills,
Thy woods and templed hills;
My heart with rapture thrills
like that above.

Let music swell the breeze,
and ring from all the trees,
Sweet freedom's song:
Let mortal tongues awake;
Let all that breathe partake,
Let rocks their silence break,
the sound prolong.

Our Fathers' God, to Thee,
Author of Liberty,
To thee we sing;
Long may our land be bright
With freedom's holy light;
Protect us by Thy might,
Great God, our King!

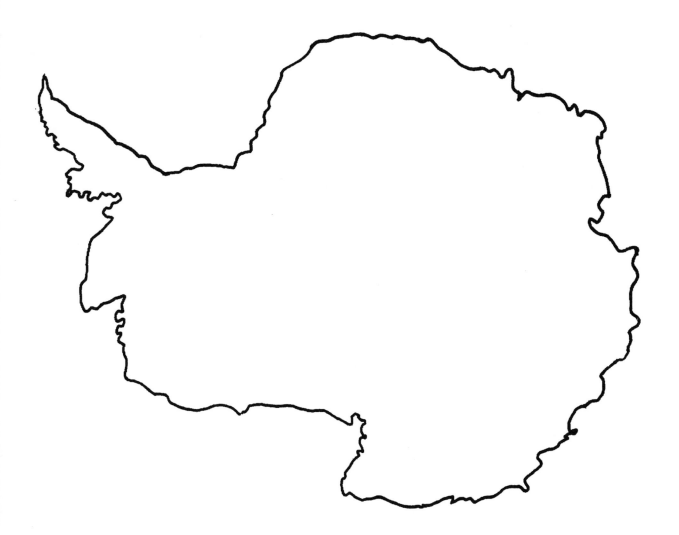

Lesson 7 - Day 2

Stillwater Morning Chronicle

Admiral Drake Sends Penguin To Mr. Popper

Early this morning, local resident, Mr. Popper, received an Air Express package containing a live penguin. The penguin, who Mr. Popper has affectionately named Captain Cook, was sent from Antarctica as a gift from Admiral Drake.

Neighbors of Mr. Popper are both curious and excited about the new addition to the town. "We'll all do our best to make the Captain feel at home!" exclaimed one neighbor.

Mr. Popper with his new pet, Captain Cook.

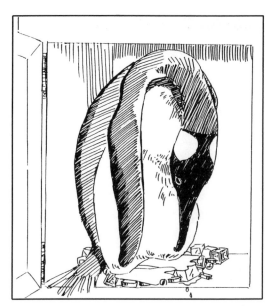

Paul Bunyan and the Whistlin' River
Retold by Linda Fowler

Maybe you've never heard of the Whistlin' River—but there was a time when it was known as the orneriest river ever to run between two banks. Some people say it was twisty and turny because it was always lookin' for trouble. Course, that was before the day it decided to get just a little too persnickety for its own good.

The Whistlin' River came by its name honestly, because every mornin' at 5:17 on the dot, and every evenin' at 6:22, just as regular as clock-work, it'd sit back on its haunches, draw itself up til it was about 203 feet tall, and let loose a piercing whistle that could be heard 679 miles in every direction.

Now, if one man can haul a big load, it doesn't take a genius to figure that two men can haul twice as much. Likewise, if one man can hear, say, 20 miles, two men together ought to be able to hear twice as far, right? So it was a regular practice for logging camps all the way up into Alaska to hire 2 or 12 men (as many as it took to hear the whistle without straining) whose main job was called "whistle-listener." That way everybody knew when to start work and when to quit, and all the camps ran smoothly (even on cloudy days.)

One day, though, Paul Bunyan (who was really a gentle man, and not easily provoked) sat on a small mountain next to the Whistlin' River in deep thought. That river, who as I said before was well-known to be more ornery than most, took a notion it wanted to play. But Ol' Paul was workin' hard at figurin' a way to stack his bunkhouses in such a way that they wouldn't tip over when they were full of sleeping men, even if one or two had nightmares and started to toss and turn. This was important because, as it was, the logging camp was about the size of Galveston, Texas, and all those buildings scattered around kind of ruined the wilderness scenery. Stacking the bunkhouses when they were empty was easy. Taking them down to let the men in was easy, but keeping them in neat stacks once they were full of loggers was another thing entirely.

Anyhow, it was in the middle of all this pondering that the Whistlin'

River all of a sudden hoisted itself up to a whopping 309 feet, leaned back just a little, and—pffffffffffffftttttt—squirted about 4,287 gallons of water straight into Ol' Paul's beard. Now Paul was right proud of his beard, and took care to keep pine trees and trapped eagles and boulders combed out of it regularly—so he was not happy. But he figured that if he just ignored the river it'd go away, so he lowered his head and pretended nothing had happened.

Well, this did anything but discourage that overgrown stream of water, who immediately reared up to almost 402 and 1/2 feet, took a deep breath—and ppsssssffffffffttt—let go a stream of water roughly the size of the Mississippi, complete with a batch of mud turtles, 77 large carp, and 2 very confused beavers.

That did it! Paul jumped up and let out a yell that set off a considerable landslide deep in the Rockies and startled a flock of ducks in Canada (who, as a result, arrived in the South months before they should've.) "Well, I never!" said Paul, exclaiming and spitting all at the same time. "I declare I never saw such a fresh river!" he said. "Don't you know who you're squirting!" He stomped around, waving his arms, for a couple of hours—which totally tickled the Whistlin' River as it settled back into its banks with a contented sigh.

Eventually Paul got back to his deep thinkin', but this time his thoughts were on teaching that uppity river a lesson. It didn't take too long (about 2 days and 27 hours) for Ol' Paul, being a poetic sort of fellow, to decide that the best course of action would be to remove the river's kinks—which would naturally straighten it out. But even though his good friend Babe, the blue ox, was plenty strong enough to pull the twists and turns out of the river, it's a well-known fact that ordinary logging chains and skid hooks do not hold water. So he needed to figure out how in tarnation to hook Babe to the swollen stream, and that required a few more hours of heavy—VERY heavy—pondering.

When the idea finally dawned, it was so simple that Paul was ashamed he'd taken so long to think of it. That very minute he and Babe took out for the North Pole, covering the distance in long strides that caused windstorms all along the way.

The closer they got to the Pole, the more blizzard tracks they began to see, and it wasn't long til Paul could tell they had reached the summer feeding grounds of all great winter storms. He lowered a sack of supplies from his shoulder and quickly set to constructing a huge box trap, which he carefully baited with fresh icicles. Then he and Babe tiptoed 40 or 50 miles back to enjoy their lunch and wait.

Wasn't long until they heard a commotion in the direction of their trap, but they waited just a little longer to make sure that whatever it was got caught for sure. Then they walked back quietly (so as not to spook their catch), peeked in, and were happy to see that they'd captured two very healthy, half-grown blizzards. It was a little tricky gettin' those fellows into his sack, but Paul was determined. Then he and Babe raced back to camp in record time, (this time triggering wind-storms that threatened to level whole towns along the way).

Before dinner that night, Paul tethered his young blizzards on either side of the pesky o' Whistlin' River, knowing full well they would do their job by morning. And sure enough, they did. When he strolled down to the riverbank after a light breakfast of 2 boxcars of sourdough pancakes (if ever a man loved flapjacks hot off the griddle, it was Paul Bunyan) and plenty of maple syrup, he found that river frozen solid.

From there, it was a simple thing to wrap a logging chain around the foot of the river about 51 times, hook the other end to Babe's harness, and holler at the Ox to "Pull!" That faithful animal, strong as it was, strained and grunted and groaned against the load. It dug its hooves into the ground and heaved with everything it had—but they didn't call that river ornery for nothing! It wouldn't budge.

Finally, Paul himself had to take hold of the chain and give it a good, strong yank. That, along with Babe's great strength, did the trick and the twisty, turny Whistlin' River was suddenly straight as a board. Course, this presented a new problem because with all the kinks out, the river was not three times longer than it had been.

Luckily, Paul had anticipated this turn of events and had already sent some of his men back to camp to fetch his great cross-cut saw and some baling wire. When they returned, he began sawing the river into 9-mile lengths, carefully rolling each section like linoleum and tying it with the wire.

Now, all this truly did take some starch out of the Whistlin' River's attitude—some say it never mustered the gumption to whistle again. And even though loggers all over the country had to look for new ways to signal their startin' and quittin' times, in the end everybody benefited.

You see, over the next 50 or 60 years Paul took special care to deliver sections of river to any logging camp that had need of more water—for cooking, drinking, or floatin' logs to the mill. As a matter of fact, some say it was rolls from the Whistlin' River that made logging the forests of Texas possible—but that's another story.

YOUR TALL TALE TITLE

HERO/HEROINE

SETTING/LOCATION

PROBLEMS

OTHER CHARACTERS

HOW THE HERO/HEROINE SOLVES THE PROBLEM

Lesson 16 - Day 4

Used by permission from *Color the Patriotic Classics.* One in the series of historical books and musical cassette tapes from *Color the Classics* by Carmen Ziarkowski.

America, the Beautiful
Katharine Lee Bates
1859-1929

Katharine Lee Bates was born August 12, 1859, in Falmouth, Massachusetts. As the daughter of a pastor, she was raised during a time in history when studying God's word was more important than math or science. She knew her scriptures well because she spent much of her youth memorizing them. As a young girl she developed an extensive vocabulary. While other children were outside playing, Katharine, who loved the English language, chose to stay inside to read her books.

It was the summer of 1893, school was out and there would be no more English classes for 3 months. Katharine and a group of other teachers traveled to Colorado to see the expanding West. Along the way, they attended the *World's Fair* in Chicago.

The World's Fair of 1893 was known as The White City for its white lights and white buildings. The ten-million dollar fair was more than anyone could have ever imagined. Countries from around the world were invited to participate. The lagoons and canals of Venice were replicated on six square-miles of swampy land. It was so huge that people did not know where to start or where to go.

After the exposition in Chicago, Katharine and her group went to Pike's Peak in Colorado. She saw deep purple mountains against a turquoise sky, fields of grain, and immense open plains. She said, "It was there, as I was looking out over the sea-like expanse of fertile country spreading away so far under ample skies, that the opening lines of this text formed themselves in my mind."

Later that evening, she and her fellow teachers discussed the trip through Chicago, the mountain climbing, and the breath-taking view they had just experienced. The whole sleepy group retired for the evening, except for Katharine, who could not fall asleep.

She took a pencil and paper and found herself writing about the events of the day in poetic form. The words naturally formed themselves into **_C.M.D._***

As she remembered the mountains she thought of Isaiah:

"How beautiful upon the mountains are the feet
of him that bringeth good tidings of peace."

The memorization of scripture as a child helped her to construe:

"O beautiful, for pilgrim feet,
whose stern impassioned stress.
A thoroughfare for freedom beat,
across the wilderness."

She completed the poem and placed it in her notebook. Six years later, in 1899, she found the poem, rewrote the text to simplify it and sent it to a publisher in Boston. The hymn was printed in the *Congregationalist*. Katharine received many letters suggesting she put her words to music. She asked composers to send in tunes. She received sixty tunes but not one fit the words. Later, in 1926, the "National Federation of Music Clubs" held a contest to set the poem to a new tune. Nine hundred entries were sent. None were acceptable and no prize was awarded. The tune we sing today is known as Materna. A New Jersey businessman named Samuel Ward, wrote the tune 10 years before Katharine's text. No one knows how Ward's tune and Bates' poem were coupled but it is the only version we sing today.

* C.M.D: Common Meter Doubled. A hymn where first and third lines are 8 syllables each and second and fourth lines are 6 syllables each. The pattern is then repeated.

Used by permission from *Color the Patriotic Classics.* One in the series of historical books and
musical cassette tapes from *Color the Classics* by Carmen Ziarkowski.

The History Of Strawberry Girl
by Wanda Fisher

Connecticut Yankee Lois Lenski did not grow up dreaming of becoming a writer. She wanted to draw. She spent hours copying photographs and magazine covers, while her father indulged her budding creativity with a new box of water colors.

Later the secret world of books began to entice her. Kate Douglas Wiggin, Louisa May Alcott, and Frances Burnett were her mentors. Still, the tug of the world of art captured her fancy.

She was a practical woman, too, being taught at a young age that work was good and excellence was a goal to strive for. She took design courses at college and learned how to draw a house plan, how to hand-letter, and how to draw cartoons. But what she loved most was drawing children.

Everywhere she went, she carried a sketch book -- and a note book. She was a meticulous, dutiful journalist, capturing moods on faces and emotions in words. Instead of picturing herself as merely an illustrator of other peoples' ideas, friends encouraged her to come up with her own stories. It was good advice.

Her lifelong habit of studying people led her to first develop only books on children of the past. She was an avid researcher; however, she soon tired of knowing people only second-hand. She wanted to write about real life and real people. After making several trips to the South, she began to realize just how diverse America was.

She came up with the idea of a series of regional books, exploring how children lived in different parts of the country. Her second regional book was <u>Strawberry Girl</u>. Lois Lenski wanted to accurately portray the world of the Florida "Cracker," and she carried out her research in a very unobtrusive way. To do research for <u>Strawberry Girl</u>, she traveled with a County Health nurse who was doing a survey of her maternity patients north of Lakeland. Lois would accompany her and store her impressions of the people -- how they spoke, dressed, lived -- and record them when alone.

Mrs. Lenski soon discovered that the world of the Florida strawberry farmer relied on three things to insure success -- the soil, the mild Central Florida winter, and...Mr. Henry Plant. The first strawberry plants in Florida may have been set as early as 1881, when settlers from Mississippi (seeking a milder climate) were astounded at the rich dark top-soil around Polk County, that was said to be six feet deep! These delicate plants could be set out in the fall, and could begin being harvested as early as January. Soon, the strawberry's fame began to spread and neighbors were trading runners with each other, and a new industry was birthed.

But success led to other problems. Soon, so many strawberries were being grown, that a way had to be found to transport them to other markets quickly. The problem was solved, however, by the farsightedness of industrialist Henry B. Plant, another Connecticut Yankee, whose Central Florida railroad line connected the east and west coast of Florida. Tampa boomed; and the delicate fruit of the strawberry could now be picked, sold for cash at Farmer's Markets, and be transported (packed in ice) to excited buyers in the North. Strawberry growing was at first a family business since they required hand labor and farms could easily be managed by one family. The "Strawberry School" was soon developed, since it would close and allow students to harvest the fruit during the months of January, February, and March. If frost threatened, the whole family would work together to cover the delicate plants with straw.

This was the world of the Boyers that Lois Lenski captured for us in <u>Strawberry Girl</u>, which won her a Newbery Award in 1946. It was a rural, bound-to-the-earth existence, yet rich in love. It was that world that captured Mrs. Lenski and persuaded her to spend her latter years in her "adopted" homeland, Florida.

Bibliography

Bruton, Quintilla. Plant City: Its Origin and History. Oviedo, Florida: Hunter/ Nickler, 1984.

Commire, Ann, ed. Something About the Author, Vol. 26. Detroit, Michigan: Gale Research Company, 1982.

Copeland, Lecilla and J.E. Dowell. La Florida: Its Land and People. Austin, Texas: The Steck Company, 1957.

Huck, Charlotte S. Authors and Illustrators of Children's Books. New York: R.R. Bowkers, 1972.

Lenski, Lois. Journey Into Childhood, Autobiography of Lois Lenski. New York: Lippincott, 1972.

Cracker Girl
by Lois Lenski

I am a little cracker girl.
You've heard of the Florida Crackers?
Well, that's us.
Ma and Pa and five of us young uns.

Pa got us a house and a stretch o ground,
and we had us some cattle,
   a good milk cow
   a horse
   and a mule.

Right from the start we was fixin'
To make us a good livin'
a-sellin' strawberries,
   oranges,
   sweet 'taters
   and sugar cane.
We plowed our field and fenced it,
We planted berries there.
We fought to keep the hogs out
   as hard as we could dare.

Our neighbors made a ruckus.
Them Slaters made a fuss.
But Ma --
 she was the one to show 'em.
Our way, it was the best.

Selection reprinted from *Florida, My Florida* by
permission of the Lois Lenski Covey Foundation, Inc.

176

Beholden
by Lois Lenski

Hit pulled my heart out nearly
 To have to send for you;
Don't like to be beholden
 For all the good you do.

But when I'm sick and porely,
 The young uns cryin' too—
If I can't call my neighbor,
 Good Lord! What would I do?

I know we're full o meanness,
 And you been kind and good;
So let's forget our bygones
 Just like a body should.

Selection reprinted from *Florida, My Florida* by
permission of the Lois Lenski Covey Foundation, Inc.

Lesson 26 - Day 3

Salt Water Taffy

1 cup sugar
$^{3}/_{4}$ cup light corn syrup
$^{2}/_{3}$ cup water
1 tablespoon cornstarch
2 tablespoons butter or margarine
1 teaspoon salt
2 teaspoons vanilla

Butter square pan, 8x8x2 inches. In 2-quart saucepan, combine sugar, corn syrup, water, cornstarch, butter and salt. Cook over medium heat, stirring constantly, to 256° on candy thermometer (or until small amount of mixture dropped into very cold water forms a hard ball.) Remove from heat; stir in vanilla. Pour into pan.

When just cool enough to handle, pull taffy until satiny, light in color and stiff. If taffy becomes sticky, butter hands lightly. Pull into long strips, ½ inch wide. With scissors, cut strips into 1-inch pieces. Wrap pieces individually in plastic wrap or waxed paper. (Candy must be wrapped to hold shape.) Makes about 1 pound.

The Mission of John Chapman
Retold by Linda Fowler

On the day baby Chapman was born, at a time when our nation was still mostly wilderness, people remarked that the sky seemed especially blue. The air was fresh and crisp, the fields were teeming with wildflowers, and the sweet smell of apple blossoms, carried along by a gentle breeze, floated into every nook and cranny of each little cabin in the village. Truly, spring had come to Massachusetts, and everyone declared it a perfectly wonderful day to be born. But nobody—not even his mama or papa—could have imagined the great mission that lay ahead for that tiny little bundle they named John.

Johnny grew quickly (as children are apt to do), and very early on it became clear that this young fellow looked at the world just a little differently than most others his age. As a toddler—mind you, a TODDLER—he'd content himself for hours sitting in the yard, chattering with the birds as he coaxed them to take seeds and berries right out of his hand. And later, instead of romping with children from the village, he much preferred to frolic with furry little wild things who lived in the woods and fields around his home.

Now obviously, since woodland creatures were his favorite friends, Johnny absolutely refused to take up hunting when he came of age—and that, as you probably know, was completely unheard of for a farm boy at that time. As a matter of fact, folks had a pretty hard time finding anything about Johnny that they considered normal. Still, as odd as he seemed, no one ever found fault with his strong faith (his parents were careful to see that he knew the Gospel) or his kind, peaceful nature.

It was well known that a person could depend on young John Chapman to pitch in whenever anybody needed help doing something, and he often amazed neighbors with his knowledge of the medicines and remedies that could be made from different plants. But more important than all that was the cheerful way he went about doing those boring day-to-day chores most everybody else hated.

One thing he didn't enjoy though, was school! It seemed perfectly silly to Johnny to spend good daylight hours stuck inside a cramped, stuffy little building. So, even though he attended (out of respect for his parents' wishes), each day of confinement produced more and more imaginary trips into the outdoors—which is where he really wanted to be, after all.

Of course, this bothered his teacher who, first of all, didn't think daydreaming was a good thing to do in school and second, was convinced that "dreamers" could only turn into unproductive adults. He was a very practical man.

Johnny though, for his part, was perfectly content with his formal education once he learned to read well enough to understand the Bible. He already knew more about animals and plants than most adults, and he had a knack for speaking the truth in simple ways. As he grew older, he took to reading large sections of scripture out loud to his animal friends who, strangely, seemed to listen. Again, pretty odd behavior for a boy—but it was about this time that he became convinced God had a special task waiting for him...just around the corner.

The spring he turned 18 began like any other, except that for Johnny there was a strange excitement in the air—a sense of adventure so real he could almost touch it. The thought popped in his head that maybe, just maybe, it was time to strike out on his own and find his calling, that thing, whatever it was, he was so certain God wanted him to do.

Naturally, when he brought the idea to his parents it took them a few minutes to settle down, because deep inside they'd always hoped Johnny would be content to marry and raise his family close to home.

But, on the other hand, they weren't really surprised either. They knew their son well, that he'd always been happiest wandering through woods or wading in streams. Besides, it seemed that nowadays the roads and rivers carried a steady trickle of wagons and boats westward. The fact was, hundreds of reasonable people had become "dreamers," leaving everything familiar behind and traveling bravely to unknown places and new beginnings.

So they agreed—but only if Johnny would take along his brother, Nathaniel, as a traveling companion. They hoped that Nat, since he was only 11, might keep "home" in Johnny's mind so he wouldn't want to stray too far. Well, that seemed like a fine idea to Johnny, and Nat, as you might have guessed, liked it even better.

Now it happened that Uncle Ben Chapman lived in western New York, in a town named Olean, and his farm seemed as good a destination as any. So very early one morning, the boys stuffed a couple of gunny sacks with such things as a Bible, a few clothes and some food, slung the bags over their shoulders, and set out on the greatest adventure of their young lives.

They walked a very, very long time to get to Olean, but neither of the boys minded because there were so many new and wonderful things to see. At night, they often shared campfires and news with other travellers, but during the day they mostly chose to enjoy the peace of the wilderness by themselves.

One day, as they rested under a huge oak that grew beside an apple orchard, the brothers watched something unusual happen on the trail they'd been traveling. A large wagon stopped almost directly in front of them, and a family piled out. The children though, instead of frolicking through the green field, walked solemnly to the edge of the orchard—uttering not one word—and stood staring at the trees (which were still pink with sweet-smelling blossoms.) Their mama and papa stood silently, also gazing toward the orchard, till the woman turned slightly, buried her face in her husband's shoulder and wept quietly.

As quickly as it began, the little drama ended. No one ever noticed John and Nat watching from under the oak as the children were called back to their places and the family resumed its journey. But Johnny pondered the scene for weeks after. From that moment on, he became increasingly aware of the fact that, in the wilderness areas they travelled, there were NO fruit trees. There were acres and acres of fir, oak and beech trees, and some berry bushes here and there—but fruit trees appeared only in areas that had been settled for years and years. And of course, the further they walked, the further apart these settlements were.

Naturally, noticing this made Johnny remember special times at home. He thought about the heavenly scent of apple blossoms in the spring, and the crisp, sweet crunch of fresh apples in the fall. He remembered his mama stringing apples up in the kitchen to dry, so there'd be applesauce all winter, and he could almost taste the mouth-watering pies and sweet cider she made. Right then and there, Johnny decided that apples were indeed a very special gift from the Lord, and now it saddened him to think about all the hard-working, brave folks headed west with no friendly apple trees to look forward to.

At any rate, when the Chapman boys finally reached Olean the were in for a surprise. Their Uncle Ben's cabin sat empty and deserted, and word was he had packed up the year before to head for a settlement called Marietta, in Ohio. Now, believe it or not, both

Johnny and Nathaniel were completely tickled to hear this news because neither boy was ready to give up the fun of exploring quite yet.

Since it was too late in the summer to start another long journey on foot, Johnny decided to look for work there in Olean. And guess what he found. Why, a job helping a farmer with his apple orchard, of course. He couldn't have been happier, and he learned a great deal in a very short time from the kindly man.

That autumn, at harvest time, Johnny drove a wagon loaded with apples to the cider mill, and it was there that God's plan for his life began to take shape for the first time. You see, as he watched the mill slowly grind the apples and press out their juice, his eyes suddenly rested on the small mountains of squeezed pulp that littered the millyard. Why, he had never seen so many seeds in one place at one time—and it dawned on him that each and every one was actually an apple tree, just waiting for a chance to grow!

He thought back to the pioneer family he'd watched say a sad goodbye to the joys of apples before they headed west; he considered his great love of wandering and the outdoors; he looked again at the thousands of seeds, and all at once his mission in life lay before him as clearly as anything he'd ever seen before.

So it began—the kindest, gentlest, most selfless legend our country ever produced started right there in that millyard, as Johnny Chapman knelt to the task of sorting, washing, and drying apple seeds. He continued this tedious work throughout the long winter, and by spring had several good sized sacks ready to go as he and Nat set out for Ohio.

On this journey, the boys were forced to travel lighter than before because of all those seeds! No extra clothes went with them this time, and food stores were limited to a sack of corn meal (they'd become quite fond of pone.) Of course, Johnny's Bible rested inside his shirt, and he took to wearing the cooking pot on his head, like a hat, since that seemed like a logical place to carry the thing. Along the way, he handed out packets of seeds and favorite scriptures to every frontier-bound family they met, and he carefully planted a few of the precious seeds in each clearing they passed.

You can see that by the time he took leave of Nathaniel at Uncle Ben's in Marietta, his pattern was well set. And, naturally, several large orchards began to sprout in the rich, black earth around the Ohio River soon after he tramped on into the wilderness beyond.

John fulfilled his mission for over 50 years, pushing further and further west, but always returning to the Ohio River basin to tend his orchards there before beginning his circuit again. It's said that when his clothes and shoes wore out, he took to wearing a rough sack with holes cut for his head and arms, and going barefoot. The pot on his head became a trademark, and his favorite traveling companion turned out to be a big, black wolf he'd once rescued from a trap.

But as odd a character as he continued to be, this man was truly beloved by all, and everyone watched for his appearances. He preached the gospel to settlers, Indians and animals alike, and spread God's apple-blessing as far west as his legs would carry him. Yet few actually knew his name. To most everyone he was always just Johnny Appleseed.

Lessons 32 & 33 - Days 1 & 2

Winston Churchill Announces New Administration
1940

Last Friday Evening I received His Majesty's commission to form a new administration. It was the wish of Parliament and the nation that this should include all parties, both those who supported the late Government and also the parties of the Opposition. I have completed the most important part of this task. A War Cabinet has been formed of five Members, representing the unity of the nation. The three party leaders have agreed to serve, either in the War Cabinet or in high executive office. The three fighting services have been filled. It was necessary that this should be done in one single day, on account of the extreme urgency and rigor of events.

Julius Caesar Objects to Illegal Execution
of The Captured Conspirators
(63 B.C.)

It is the duty of all men, Roman Senators, in their discussions on subjects that are difficult to decide, to strip themselves of hatred and affection, of revenge and pity. When the mind is clouded with such emotions it cannot easily determine the truth; no man has ever followed these emotions and at the same time made a wise decision. When we exercise our judgement only, that is best. Hatred, revenge, and pity can overpower our thinking and we will lose our good judgement. I could tell you a great many examples of kings and other leaders who made foolish decisions because of their resentment or compassion. I would rather tell you the example of our forefathers and show you how they acted differently than their impulses and emotions. They agreed to act wisely and with sound judgement.

How to Open a Door

Doors are important to all of us. They help us feel safe, they keep out the rain, and they provide privacy. Sometimes, however, we need to change the position of a door from being closed to being open. Today, I am going to show you the proper way to open one of these fabulous inventions.

The first step is to walk up to the door. You must be closer than an arm's length to properly follow these steps. (Speaker walks to the demonstration door and extends arm.)

The second step is to firmly grasp the door knob. A firm grip ensures success in the next phase of door opening. (Speaker grasps door knob.)

Now turn the door knob using wrist action to complete the turn. (Speaker turns the knob.)

The final step has a bit of a twist to it, as each door has its own manner of opening. You must determine the type of door with which you are working in order to complete this final phase. Either push or pull the door to open it. (Speaker opens the demonstration door.)

As you can see, the door is open now and people can easily pass through it. I hope you will follow these simple steps next time you need to change the position of a door in your home. And don't forget to be thankful for these very useful items in our lives.

Lesson 34

Used by permission from *Color the Patriotic Classics.* One in the series of historical books and musical cassette tapes from *Color the Classics* by Carmen Ziarkowski.

The Star-Spangled Banner
Francis Scott Key
1779-1843

Francis Scott Key lived on a 3000 acre farm called *Tierra Rubra* (Red Land) in Frederick (now called Carroll) County, Maryland. Francis was raised to rely upon God's word for everything in his life. His mother was instrumental in imparting the scriptures over everyday issues.

Francis learned much from his blind grandmother. She not only taught Francis to pray, but was also responsible for teaching him to speak in a soft and clear manner. She was the inspiration for his excellent speaking ability which proved to be a tremendous skill for Francis later in life.

Francis studied law under the advice of his uncle Philip. He became the most popular lawyer in Maryland. By the time he was 27 years old, he was in great demand. Francis married the beautiful *Mary Taylor Lloyd*, who gave him 11 children.

By 1814, Britain had been at war with America for two years. Washington D.C. had been captured and burned in August. Later that fall, the British fleet surrounded the Americans in Chesapeake Bay. British Admiral Cochrane had informed secretary Monroe that Fort McHenry, the fort that guarded the narrow entrance into the harbor and secured Baltimore, was about to be destroyed. The British plan was to disable Fort McHenry and then attack Baltimore. *Dr. Beanes*, a prominent physician and a close friend of Francis Scott Key was captured.

Francis, determined to obtain his friend's release, sought President Madison for the proper paperwork. President Madison knew about Key's persuasive abilities and granted him whatever he needed. Key and *Colonel Skinner*, sailed under a flag of truce to the *Tonnant*, the admiral's ship. Once on board, Key requested the release of the doctor. Within minutes, Key realized he had chosen the wrong day. This was the day that Admiral Cochrane had selected to attack Fort McHenry. Cochrane refused to return the physician, Francis Key or Colonel Skinner before the planned attack.

Admiral Cochrane received bad news. His land forces attacking the city had been driven back with many casualties. He was told that unless Fort McHenry was captured or completely destroyed, the whole campaign would be lost.

The news that this crusade would soon be lost was followed by fierce bombardment. The shelling started at daybreak on the 13th of September, 1814 and continued through the night. Sixteen British frigates took part in the bombing. Fifteen to eighteen hundred rounds were fired. It was a tiresome night. Key, Skinner and Dr. Beanes anxiously waited as they watched the attack.

Key had been told by British sailors to take a good look at his precious flag because it would not be there by morning. Key could not take his eyes off the fort which was attacked be land and by sea. The disheartened Americans were desperately trying to retaliate but the 42-pound cannons could not reach the British ships. Cannon ball after cannon ball left the American fort only to dive straight into the water before the fleet. Admiral Cochrane was quite confident that the fort would be taken easily. He was anxious to finish off this job so that he could destroy the rest of Maryland.

By early morning there was great silence and Key was slowly giving up hope. Through the smoke of battle and the early morning mist, he grabbed a pair of field glasses and looked toward the fort 2½ miles away. Would the waving flag be American or British? One can only imagine the thoughts that ran through Key's mind. He gasped as he saw the 15-starred flag still waving. The Americans had not surrendered. After the shelling of 1800 rounds, our flag had received 11 holes and only 4 out of 1,000 men died in the fort. When all the smoke had cleared, history recorded that a small poorly-equipped army of men had fought and won against the greatest army and navy in the world.

Francis took a letter from his pocket and quickly jotted down a few stanzas. Having received word of total defeat, the British, had no choice but to return Francis Key, Colonel Skinner and Dr. Beanes back to Maryland. That night, in a local hotel, Key finished his poem. The following morning he showed it to his brother-in-law, Judge Joseph Nicholson, who had been second-in-command at Fort McHenry and lived through the bombardment.

The poem called *"The Defense of Fort McHenry,"* first appeared in the Baltimore newspaper, *American.* People liked it and began to sing it to a tune that allegedly came from an old drinking song in England called, *"To Anacreon In Heaven."* One reason for its popularity was that the colonists already knew the tune. The Star-Spangled Banner was not accepted formally as our national anthem until Herbert Hoover signed a law in 1931.

Used by permission from *Color the Patriotic Classics.* One in the series of historical books and musical cassette tapes from *Color the Classics* by Carmen Ziarkowski.

Skills Index

189

Skills Index

Bibliography

Atwater, Richard & Florence. *Mr. Popper's Penguins*. Boston: Little, Brown and Company, 1938.

Eaton, Jeannette. *David Livingstone – Foe of Darkness*. William Morrow & Co., Inc., 1947.

Lenski, Lois. *Strawberry Girl*. New York: Bantam Doubleday Dell Publishing Group, Inc., 1945.

White, E.B. *The Trumpet of the Swan*. Harper Collins Publishers.

Yates, Elizabeth. *Amos Fortune: Free Man*. New York: Penguin Books USA Inc., 1950.

Ziarkowski, Carmen. *Color the Classics*. P.O. Box 440, Silver Springs, NY 14550.